BUILDING COMMUNITY

Also published by The Graduate School Press of Syracuse University

Pedagogy, not Policing
Positive Approaches to Academic
Integrity at the University

Interrupting Heteronormativity
Lesbian, Gay, Bisexual and Transgender Pedagogy
and Responsible Teaching at Syracuse University

Building Pedagogical Curb Cuts
Incorporating Disability in the University
Classroom and Curriculum

Using Writing to Teach

BUILDING COMMUNITY
Stories and Strategies for
Future Learning Community
Faculty and Professionals

Edited by
Terra Peckskamp
and Carrie McLaughlin

The Graduate School Press
SYRACUSE UNIVERSITY

Copyright © 2010 The Graduate School Press of Syracuse University
Syracuse, New York 13244

Library of Congress Cataloging-in-Publication Data

Building community : stories and strategies for future learning community faculty and
professionals / edited by Terra Peckskamp and Carrie McLaughlin.
    p. cm.
    Includes bibliographical references and index.
    ISBN-13: 978-0-9777847-3-8 (pbk.)
    ISBN-10: 0-9777847-3-8 (pbk.)
    1. Group work in education--United States--Case studies. 2. College teaching--United States--
Case studies. 3. Professional learning communities--United States--Case studies. 4.
Interdisciplinary approach in education--United States--Case studies. I. Peckskamp, Terra, 1971-
II. McLaughlin, Carrie, 1971-
    LB1032.B82 2010
    378.1'76--dc22
                                        2010022815

For more information about this publication, please contact

The Graduate School Press
220 Bowne Hall
Syracuse University
Syracuse, NY 13244

www.syr.edu/gradschool/gsprograms/resources/gradschoolpress.html

Manufactured in the United States of America

Contents

Acknowledgments

WE are grateful for the opportunity provided by the Graduate School at Syracuse University to work on this project and gain valuable skills in serving as editors for this book. Thanks to Dr. Stacey Lane Tice and Sandra Hurd, past Interim Dean of the Graduate School, for their support of this project.

We would like to thank Lori Foster, who served as our copy editor. She provided great insight and attention to detail in reviewing each chapter of this book. We would especially like to recognize Ken Sagendorf for his work in the Graduate School and in guiding the early stages of the project. Special thanks to Siera Miller, Carren Jao, and Chris Calvert-Minor for their work preparing the index. Most importantly, we would like to thank Glenn D. Wright, Assistant Director for Graduate School Programs in the Graduate School, for the time and energy he dedicated to keeping us on track and getting this book published.

Our deepest thanks go to members of our advisory board—Alexei Abrahams, Cathy Engstrom, Sandra Hurd, Jennah Jones, Pat Rummel, Ken Sagendorf, Rachel Smith, Stacey Lane Tice, Vincent Tinto, Barry Wells, and Bobbi Yonai—for their insight and support. Their knowledge of learning communities and experience in professional practice and graduate teaching helped us understand the needs of future practitioners and proved invaluable as we thought through the purpose and goals of this project.

We hope that as you read this book you will discover ways in which your work with students can be enhanced by the experiences shared in these pages. It is a privilege to work with college students, and doing so in ways that serve them better makes our collective work that much stronger. It is our hope that this book will give you reason to engage thoughtfully and courageously in the learning community efforts on your campus.

BUILDING COMMUNITY

Editors' Introduction

Terra Peckskamp and Carrie McLaughlin

THE late 1990s were a time when faculty and staff at Syracuse University (SU) were examining ways to make a positive impact on student learning and satisfaction, and to create an SU "Signature Experience." In 1998 the Whitman School of Management, the Honors Program, and the Office of Residence Life conducted a small pilot project that placed 43 students in two learning communities (Management and Honors). "Supported by experience and research," wrote then–Vice President for Undergraduate Studies Ronald R. Cavanagh in a memo describing the effort, "it is our assumption that students learn lessons faster and retain them longer when these lessons are reinforced by linked or networked learning environments cutting across the curricula and the co-curricula." Nine years later, in the 2007–2008 academic year, there were over 1,600 students participating in 42 learning communities and lifestyle housing options. In addition, over 200 faculty members, staff, paraprofessional students, and administrators participate in the coordination of learning community programs.

Learning communities are often used as one strategy in an institution's effort to improve undergraduate student success (Shapiro and Levine, 1999, p. 15). Learning communities can positively influence student intellectual and social development, leading to greater student satisfaction with their undergraduate experience, and, on a grander scale, they can even serve as a factor in the reinvention of undergraduate education (Shapiro and Levine, 1999, p. 171). As demonstrated through assessment projects, learning communities at SU help ease first-year student transitions by making a large campus more navigable, creating a more academically and socially supportive residential environment, and creating connections among and between students, faculty, and staff.

Successful learning communities require the participation and support of many different campus stakeholders, including academic departments; the registrar; housing, residence life, and admissions offices; and others. Indeed,

Cavanagh and his colleagues cited the benefits of such collaboration for the larger institutional culture when formally proposing the creation of a permanent learning communities program at SU: "Collaboration and shared responsibility among faculty and professional staff in Academic and Student Affairs promotes a sharing of best practices, curricular coherence, and the integration of student developmental planning. Providing these opportunities for integration benefits everyone."[1] But creating a learning community program that has a positive impact on students, engages faculty, and is well coordinated is no easy task, and there are many stories of challenges and success along the way. The purpose of this book is to share some of these stories.

The book is divided into two sections. The first part, "History, Structure, and Assessment," provides an overview of learning communities. In the first chapter, "Understanding the Evolution of Learning Community Concepts: A Historical Perspective," Dianna Winslow presents a historical survey of learning communities, going back to John Dewey and Alexander Meiklejohn in the 1920s and the debates about general education. Various learning community structures and models are discussed by Heather Strine Patterson in "Learning Communities: A Structural Overview." jared halter and Camila Lértora Nardozzi address learning community assessment in their chapter, "Tips and Strategies for Assessing Learning Communities." Finally, W. Leslie Burleson and Michele Tarnow present stories gathered from a qualitative learning community assessment project at Syracuse University in "Learning Communities Assessment: Challenges and Recommendations from Faculty and Staff Perspectives."

Part Two, "Teaching and Learning in a Learning Community," builds on the structural groundwork of the first section by presenting individual stories about learning community experiences, as students and faculty members share their insights on learning communities' impact on various aspects of teaching and learning. Eileen Strempel examines the effort to build community in a classroom in "The Arts Adventure LC: A Classroom-to-Community Cultural Connection." Eric Alderman explores the challenges of creating a learning community from scratch in "Creating a Unique Learning Community Through Creativity, Innovation, and Entrepreneurship." Extending the theme of teaching and learning, Silvio Torres-Saillant and James Duah-Agyeman delve into what it means to create a learning environment where difficult conversations can be had in "Diversity and Citizenship."

Paul Buckley, a graduate student when he wrote "Creating Change and Continuity in Your Learning Community," discusses the challenges of coordinating a learning community while pursuing an advanced degree, and Jamie Kathleen Portillo considers the rewards and difficulties of teaching in a

---

[1] Quoted from a 1999 document prepared for the Office of the Vice Chancellor.

learning community as a graduate student in "Learning Community Encounters and Strategies for Effective Teaching Assistantship." Braden and Rachel Smith, who were both undergraduate participants in a learning community and later taught in learning communities as graduate students, bring their unique perspective to bear in "Bridging the Gap: Constructing Faculty–Student Relationships for Mutual Learning." Maria Lopez also took part in a learning community, but as a graduate student, and reflects on her experience in "The Higher Education Learning Community of Syracuse University: A Participant's Perspective." Chris Calvert-Minor contemplates what graduate education might look like if there were more graduate student–focused learning communities in "Through the Looking Glass of Undergraduate Learning Communities (And What the Graduate Student Finds)."

A number of strategies for implementing a successful learning community are offered by Elizabeth Occhino and Jennifer Kellington in "The Mary Ann Shaw Center for Public and Community Service: Lessons Learned." One of these strategies is student mentoring, the subject of "Mentoring and the Gateway Learning Community: The Importance of Mentoring in Providing Access to Social Capital" by Larry Thomas and Nicole Zervas Adsitt. Jennah Jones and Joshua Lawrie conclude the expository chapters by comparing and contrasting two learning community experiences in "Institutional Pedagogies: Exploring Two Learning Community Programs." The final contribution, "Critical Learning Community Resources for Educating Campus Stakeholders," by Terra Peckskamp and Joshua McIntosh, summarizes additional learning community resources.

This book offers a snapshot of the learning community stories and experiences of Syracuse University students, faculty, and staff. These stories offer insight, humor, and useful strategies, and together they provide a wonderful look into the learning community world. We hope that you will be able to connect with these stories and that they can be used to inform your own teaching and learning.

References

Shapiro, N. S., & Levine, J. H. (1999). *Creating learning communities: A practical guide for winning support, organizing for change, and implementing programs*. San Francisco: Jossey-Bass.

Introduction

Sandra Hurd

ONE measure of a university program that has "arrived" is its mention in publications that provide prospective students and their families with national rankings. By that measure, learning communities—although they have been around in various forms for decades—have finally arrived. The first national rankings of learning community programs appeared in *U.S. News and World Report* in 2001, and Syracuse University can be justifiably proud that its learning community program has been ranked ever since.

Why are learning communities so important in higher education today? And why is it important to offer students—particularly first-time, first-year students—the opportunity to participate in learning communities? A college or university, especially a large one, is a complex and often intimidating environment, both socially and academically, for an incoming student. In those critical first few days, when many of the attitudes and values students carry with them throughout their undergraduate careers take root, learning communities give students a way to become immediately connected and engaged. And contemplating life with thirty or more strangers produces much less anxiety when students know they share common ground upon which to build relationships. In addition to promoting social integration, learning communities promote academic success by providing a network of peers with whom to study and share academic experiences, by creating connections with faculty and staff, and by blurring the lines between learning in and out of the classroom.

But it is not only students who benefit from learning communities. Faculty and staff who work with learning communities report that they both enjoy the experience and learn a great deal from collaboration that crosses the sometimes seemingly impermeable boundaries between academic affairs and student affairs, as well as boundaries between the disciplines. They also enjoy the kind of boundary crossing that happens as they connect multiple kinds of learning experiences to develop a more holistic learning environment for students.

4

Syracuse University clearly benefits as well from greater student satisfaction and an improved academic climate. In 2004, SU participated in the National Study of Living-Learning Programs (NSLLP). The results of that survey show that SU students who participate in learning communities are more likely than non-participants to find the residence hall climate academically and socially supportive; to spend time discussing sociocultural issues with peers; to desire involvement in research; to be part of student clubs/groups; to enjoy challenging academic pursuits; and to have a sense of civic engagement. These are all outcomes that lead to deeper learning and greater student success.

It is my hope that what you learn from this book intrigues you and sparks your interest in finding out more about learning communities. Whether you are in the academy for only a short time or want to make teaching your life's work, participating in a learning community can be a wonderful and very rewarding experience.

Part One

History, Structure, and Assessment

Understanding the Evolution of Learning Community Concepts
A Historical Perspective

Dianna Winslow

GENERALLY, institutions intend for learning communities and linked courses to provide academic and social connections that encourage peer support for students early in their academic careers. Such connections increase student retention by creating friendships that produce environments conducive to academic success and promote an academic basis for socialization. The common element of learning community courses is that a fixed population of students live together and attend one or more classes together for a specified period of time, usually one or two semesters.[1] The writing on learning communities has been helpful in understanding the value of curricular cohesion and academically based socialization for student success. Throughout the twentieth century, many colleges and universities experimented with these ideas, creating residential learning communities, work-learning internship programs (the precursor of service learning), and interdisciplinary approaches to lower-division programs of study. This is, at least in part, the historical basis for learning community design. A historical perspective on the development of these concepts and their foundations is important to helping students succeed in this evolving university environment.

A Link to the Past

Learning communities as we currently practice them might be considered a variation on ideas that have surfaced and resurfaced in education literature

---

[1] The work of Faith Gabelnick, Jean MacGregor, Roberta S. Matthews and Barbara Leigh Smith on learning community history, conception, and implementation is instrumental in understanding the range of possibilities for linking courses to encourage active and dynamic educational explorations and outcomes.

since the beginning of the twentieth century. The philosophies of John Dewey and Alexander Meiklejohn figured largely in the debates of the 1920s about what general education should encompass for first- and second-year university students. These historical debates are particularly pertinent to understanding a genealogy of development for learning communities in their many forms. Ideas that emerged from these early investigations have helped to shape current undergraduate education, including learning and living communities like those at Syracuse University. John Dewey's scholarship on the inherently social nature of human learning has informed and continues to inform current teaching methodology.

Dewey focuses primarily on theories of learning and knowing: how learning happens most effectively; how physical environment and activity affect learning acquisition; how socially organized learning situations enhance "knowing" and active, curious inquiry. In *Schools of Tomorrow*, first published in 1915, Dewey, with his daughter Evelyn Dewey, writes of human experience as inescapably social. It follows that learning is most productive and knowledge is made in social situations with emotional, moral, and practical social problems to solve: "Knowledge that is worthy of being called knowledge, training of the intellect that is sure to amount to anything, is obtained only by participating intimately and actively in activities of social life" (Dewey & Dewey, 1915/1962, p. 47). Dewey's collaborative approaches to teaching and learning express his commitment to teach about social control and community life, since that is how humans live and, consequently, learn (Gabelnick, MacGregor, Matthews & Smith, 1990, p. 16).

Dewey points out that as a society we value a very small portion of learning; learning done in schools carries a high premium while we virtually ignore the vast amount of learning taking place in the day-to-day lives of students doing the learning. He suggests looking to the larger educational forum of learning in daily life (which is stimulated by emerging daily needs) to establish theory and method for teaching within the walls of the classroom. Dewey also observes that most schooling is about the accumulation of others' knowledge without the student creating a relationship with that knowledge for him or herself; information is learned by rote and does not involve the student's judgment in analyzing that information for correctness or usefulness to a task to which it is being applied. In the 1970s, Paulo Freire called this the "banking" model of learning (1993, p. 53–54), where instructors make "deposits" into the heads of students, but the knowledge being deposited has not been chosen for particular students or the contexts in which they are learning. Dewey (and later Freire) promoted learning as a student-centered process—a cooperative, active inquiry focused on finding solutions to real problems:

Probably the greatest and commonest mistake that we all make is to forget that learning is a necessary incident of dealing with real situations.... [B]y the conventional method of teaching, the pupil learns maps instead of the world—the symbol instead of the fact.... To find out how to make knowledge when it is needed is the true end of the acquisition of information in school, not the information itself. (Dewey & Dewey, 1915/1962, pp. 3, 13)

Dewey's concepts are easily recognizable in learning community pedagogy, and in university classrooms generally. A "good" educational experience supports Dewey's theories about learning being inextricably social by extensively using group work, peer review, and student-driven inquiry. In my field of study, some composition instructors use popular culture as a lens for rhetorical analysis to bring the world "out there" right into the classroom; this involves students in thinking about the images and situations that confront them on a daily basis, creating continuity between their "school" learning and their lives. Service learning–based college curricula look to the "larger educational forum of learning in daily life" as a means of applying classroom learning to real-world objectives. Again, within composition and rhetoric, many composition instructors are moving toward a student-centered classroom experience; the role of teacher-as-expert begins to melt into co-authorship of knowing. Both teachers and students "find out how to make knowledge when it is needed" (Dewey & Dewey, 1915/1962, p. 13), rather than the teacher depositing information into students' empty heads. The push for critical thinking in general education classes attempts to address the same idea.

While Dewey's theorizing and experimentation focused on the learning process and development of the individual through collaborative learning environments, Alexander Meiklejohn pursued experimental curricular designs and programmatic structures of institution learning, focusing on the first two years of university education. Meiklejohn firmly advocated for a two-year undergraduate integrated program, and implemented his ideas when he instituted the Experimental College at the University of Wisconsin in 1927. For two years, first- and second-year students worked with classic texts on ancient Greek civilization, comparing them with modern American works that illuminated American society. The goal was not to have the students memorize facts about Athenian society, nor was it to acquaint them with particular works of American literature their instructors found important. Rather, Meiklejohn and his colleagues used the texts as vehicles for prompting students to evaluate their own society, drawing on and extending what they already knew. Using reading as the informational foundation, students were asked to "look into the situation with which [Athens] was dealing; put yourself into [its] place; write a paper and tell what you would have done" (Meiklejohn, 1932, p. 55). Students were asked to use writing and discussion to "get their minds active, to give them a sense of the urgency of human need, to establish in them the activity of seeing and solving problems" (pp. 56–57). Meiklejohn felt that studying Western civilization was "simply a device for stirring a[n American college student] to see that with which he is already acquainted, to think about what he knows" (p. 56), and, by extension, to apply that to current social problems.[2]

Such a program would span both years, with the unit of organization not the individual departmental course, but an educational offering using instructors from many specialties and departments, exploring common readings through the lenses of their various expertise. Discussion and writing would then be grounded in comparisons between the readings and observations of students' socially lived experience, all executed using rhetorical strategies learned in the college classroom. In *Against the Current: Reform and Experimentation in Higher Education*, Richard M. Jones and Barbara Leigh Smith describe how "students' eyes were opened as they looked at their own society with the tools they acquired in college, something that traditional education had never asked them to do" (Jones & Smith, 1984, p. 11).

Meiklejohn's concept of a unified, two-year, lower-division academic program had the primary goal of nurturing social and academic community. It was his opinion that continuity of social-academic experience—shared and collaborative teaching responsibilities among a team of faculty members, consistent populations of peers class to class and subject to subject, and collaborative problem solving in course assignments—was the unifying factor in the program's curricular structure, not what was studied. According to Meiklejohn,

> a liberal education is not training in technical skill; nor is it instruction in knowledge…. [I]t implies a unity of understanding against the unrelatedness of scattered bits of knowledge … to serve men in the creation and maintenance of a social order, a scheme of individual and group living. (1932, p. xvii)

Meiklejohn and Dewey had clear beliefs about the function of a liberal education. Both were striving for educational continuity between social life and school education. Both understood that students lean into their college

---

[2] Meiklejohn is also notoriously known (to some) as the father of the "Great Books" movement in the 1940s and 1950s. University of Chicago chancellor Robert M. Hutchins initiated "The Chicago Plan," a.k.a. "The College," which is possibly the most well known of these programs. Citing Meiklejohn's educational methodologies, Hutchins orchestrated an undergraduate program based only on readings from the so-called Classics with a capital "C." Considered by many to be classist and exclusive, Meiklejohn's theories have been discredited in some scholarly circles because of this association with Hutchins' work. This study does not need to deal with the "Great Books" programs and their problems, but I do not believe that the spirit of democracy and academic inquiry to which Meiklejohn was devoted is represented by Hutchins' model.

experience with interest when connections are made with their lives in society. They were firm in their conviction: "Schools and colleges are not something apart from the social order to which they belong. They are that order trying to prepare its youth for participation in its own activities" (Meiklejohn, 1932, p. xi).

Historical Antecedents to Current Learning Communities

The twentieth century was full of experimentation based on Dewey's and Meiklejohn's ideas. Each programmatic attempt developed and refined understanding about community and collaboration as part of the learning process. All were based (as current and emerging programs are) on three common premises: the best learning takes place in relatively small, cohesive communities; learning has to be relevant to students' commitment to a world larger than the university, considering both the academy and society as sites for making knowledge; and education is at its most productive using a combination of tradition and innovation (Gamson, 2000, pp. 114–115). Dewey's comments in *How We Think* underscore this call for a methodological mix of tradition and experimentation, as he charges educators to be carefully conscious of the choices being made in designing learning situations:

> Consider the power and purposes of those being taught. It is not enough that certain materials or methods have proven effective with other individuals at other times. There must be a reason for thinking that they will function in generating an experience that has educative quality with particular individuals at a particular time. (1933, pp. 45–46)

Some of these "experiments" have endured and flourished as respected institutions of higher education. Most live on in some way, even if only by the impact they have had on current educational philosophies. Many models for experimental undergraduate education build on Alexander Meiklejohn's theories and the Experimental College at the University of Wisconsin. Though only in operation from 1927 to 1932, this program developed enduring ideas, which have been made and remade throughout the rest of the century. Current one-year general education thematic studies and honors programs at some California state universities are contemporary cousins of Meiklejohn's program, complete with the integrated theme of human civilization. John Tussman's vision for the Experimental Program at the University of California at Berkeley, which operated from 1965 to 1969, is derived directly from his exposure to Meiklejohn's ideas as an undergraduate at Wisconsin, even though it was by that time "a legend, an educational *Paradise Lost*" (Tussman, 1969, p. vii). He believed that the Experimental College "offered the solution to the central problem of undergraduate education," and he created the Experimental Program to "reincarnate [its] spirits and principles" (p. vii). The theme of this two-year program mimics Meiklejohn's almost directly, despite Tussman's disclaimer that he is "captivated, not enslaved" by Meiklejohn's Athens–America curriculum (p. 52). Tussman's curriculum explores civilization in Greece during the Peloponnesian Wars and in seventeenth-century England in the first year of the program, and in American society in the second.

Other schools played upon Meiklejohn's themes. In the 1980s, the College of the Holy Cross in central Massachusetts developed the First-Year Program, which invited students and faculty to

> join in dialogue about basic human questions: What is the moral character of learning and teaching? How do we find meaning in life and history? What are our obligations to one another? What is our special responsibility to the world's poor and powerless? (Singleton, Garvey, & Phillips, 1969/2000, p. 142)

The program's central theme was an adaptation of a question posed by Leo Tolstoy in *A Confession*—"How then shall we live?"—and each of the ten faculty team members introduced his or her disciplinary area of study through this question. Students attended small and large seminars, read common books, participated in co-curricular events, and lived in the same residence hall.

In 1972, Richmond College at City University of New York began its Integrated Studies program, which looked much like other experimental programs that emphasized knowledge-making and student-centered curricular choices. The difference here was that Richmond College was the first experimental program to work with working-class students in a major urban public university (Quart & Stacey, 2000, p. 119). Popular culture and service learning projects were used with "great" books and modern films to investigate racism, identity, capitalism, and politics. This program considered its major success "raising the level of student and faculty consciousness about the whole teaching and learning process: relations with students, the nature of governance, and the concept of knowledge" (Quart & Stacey, 2000, p. 120), harkening back to Meiklejohn's comment that "as [teachers] attempt to educate their pupils, [they] must themselves be gaining education from one another, and from their common enterprise" (1932, p. xv). Richmond College contributed to "the idea of a humane, communal, student centered education for more than the [private college] elite" (Quart & Stacey, 2000, p. 120).

The Evergreen State College in Olympia, Washington, and the University of California, Santa Cruz, on the central coast of California, both came into existence through state mandates to "develop an innovative structure that would not simply duplicate the existing academic resources of the state" (Yountz, 1984, p. 95). Tremendous need for higher education expansion in the late fifties and sixties brought both of these schools into existence, and with them a commitment to "innovative undergraduate education" that would be kept "intimate, personal, encouraging a sense of belonging" (Adams, 2000, p. 131). The many small college buildings on the University of California, Santa Cruz, campus today are a remnant of the original intention to challenge disciplinary segregation by defining individual colleges through their own "coherent and independent undergraduate curricula, based upon distinctive thematic definitions of liberal education, and emphasizing interdisciplinary courses and innovative teaching techniques" (Adams, 2000, p. 132). Evergreen, too, considers "Interdisciplinary Studies to be the centerpiece of curricular efforts," taking the opportunity in the first year to "design the strongest possible and most diverse set of Meiklejohn-like interdisciplinary programs we could conceive" (Yountz, 1984, p. 95).

Other institutions during the century were more interested in the integration of life and school, and built programs that blended Meiklejohn's ideas with Dewey's philosophies on lived experience and educational symbiosis. In 1938, Royce Stanley Pitkin took Dewey's ideas and began to shape the undergraduate curriculum of Goddard College, a small, private liberal arts college in rural Vermont. Students lived on "campus," which was a large manor house and the converted barns and outbuildings of a large country estate (Chickering, 1984, p. 303). Coursework was negotiated and designed between the student and instructor, and evaluations were narrative rather than lettered. All students took part in on-campus work-study for eight hours per week. From its original residential organization, Goddard developed an adult degree program in the sixties, serving students who had at one time gone to college but had not finished the degree. Viewing living and learning as inextricable, Goddard provided an unconventional academy for these students. They designed their own course of study and participated in unstructured on-campus study. They also participated in credit-bearing work-learning experiences off campus (comprising most of their "coursework") and came to the Vermont campus twice a year for two weeks each time. Through its many incarnations over the last sixty-plus years, this college has nurtured, and continues to nurture, students "as unique individuals who take charge of their own learning and collaborate with other students, staff, and faculty to build a strong community" (Goddard College, 2003).

To reiterate, these institutions have developed from a legacy of often radical experimentation, but not simply for innovation's sake. These programs have emerged from a deeply held educational philosophy that general college education is about more than learning known facts in diverse areas of study. They are founded on the philosophy that college, particularly in the first two years, is for teaching students how to see themselves within the context of the democratic society in which they live and work.

The above descriptions are organized to reflect certain similarities between philosophies and programs. If they are ordered chronologically, it becomes clear that exploring and implementing alternative educational possibilities is driven by educators searching for ways to accommodate the extremely dynamic definition of a democratic citizenry. These institutions were, and are, working with a rapidly changing world. Most started as "ideal" college communities, with students who were residential, mostly young, and often single. By the end of World War II, new ways of reaching older and non-residential students, some with families, had to be found. "Traditions" from experimental residential colleges and universities were adapted for older, commuting students, retaining identification with the three premises of community, commitment to the larger world, and blending what has traditionally worked in teaching and learning with experimentation to create active, student-centered education.

Many current general education pedagogical trends are supported by the results of twentieth-century undergraduate programmatic experimentation. In *Learning Communities: Creating Connections Among Students, Faculty, and Disciplines*, Gabelnick et al. see "recent work in such diverse areas as the social construction of knowledge, collaborative learning, writing and critical thinking, feminist pedagogy, and cognitive and intellectual development [that] supports and resonates with the learning community effort" as directly emerging from these experiments (1990, p. 17). Learning community work has incorporated many of these recent developments, including service learning and critical pedagogy, as pathways to student acquisition of knowledge that does work in the worlds they inhabit. With the current focus at Syracuse University on community engagement and "Scholarship in Action," course-work has moved toward student-driven inquiry and the development of critical citizens with public lives, not just students learning to attend and be successful in university lives.

References

Adams, W. (2000). Getting real: Santa Cruz and the crisis of liberal education. In D. DeZure (Ed.), *Learning from* Change: *Landmarks in teaching and learning in higher education from* Change *magazine, 1969–1999* (pp. 131–134). Sterling, VA: Stylus.

Chickering, A. W. (1984). Alternatives for the 80s: The Goddard-Pitkin legacy. In R. M. Jones & B. L. Smith (Eds.), *Against the current: Reform and experimentation in higher education* (pp. 303–319). Cambridge, MA: Schenkman.

Dewey, J. (1933). *How we think*. Lexington, MA: Heath.

Dewey, J., & Dewey, E. (1962). *Schools of tomorrow*. New York: E. P. Dutton. (Original work published 1915)

Freire, P. (1993). *Pedagogy of the oppressed*. New York: Continuum.

Gabelnick, F., MacGregor, J., Matthews, R. S., & Smith, B. L. (1990). *Learning communities: Creating connections among students, faculty, and disciplines*. New Directions for Teaching and Learning, 41. San Francisco: Jossey-Bass.

Gamson, Z. F. (2000). The origins of contemporary learning communities: Residential colleges, experimental colleges, and living and learning communities. In D. DeZure (Ed.), *Learning from Change: Landmarks in teaching and learning in higher education from* Change *Magazine, 1969–1999* (pp. 113–116). Sterling, VA: Stylus.

Goddard College. (2003, October 27). About Goddard. Retrieved March 8, 2004, from the Digital Frontier database: http://www.goddard.edu/about/missionandphilosophy.html

Jones, R. M., & Smith, B. L. (Eds.). (1984). *Against the current: Reform and experimentation in higher education*. Cambridge, MA: Schenkman.

Meiklejohn, A. (1932). *The experimental college*. New York: Harper and Brothers.

Quart, L., & Stacey, J. (2000). Innovation on Staten Island. In D. DeZure (Ed.), *Learning from* Change: *Landmarks in teaching and learning in higher education from* Change *Magazine, 1969–1999* (p. 119). Sterling, VA: Stylus.

Singleton, Jr., R. A., Garvey, R. H., & Phillips, G. A. (2000). Connecting the academic and social lives of students: The Holy Cross first-year program. In D. DeZure (Ed.), *Learning from* Change: *Landmarks in teaching and learning in higher education from* Change *Magazine, 1969–1999* (pp. 141–143). Sterling, VA: Stylus. (Original work published 1969)

Tussman, J. (1969). *Experiment at Berkeley*. New York: Oxford University Press.

Yountz, B. (1984). The Evergreen State College: An experiment maturing. In R. M. Jones & B. L. Smith (Eds.), *Against the current: Reform and experimentation in higher education* (pp. 93–118). Cambridge, MA: Schenkman.

Learning Communities

A Structural Overview

Heather Strine Patterson

RUTH Federman Stein defines learning communities as the intentional arrangement of environments inside and outside the classroom to achieve greater learning outcomes by organizing more student interactions with faculty and between students around scholarship (2004). Learning communities can have residential or non-residential and course or non-course components. However, the overarching goal of learning communities is to construct "seamless learning environments" (Kuh, 1996), where the boundaries of learning are blurred between in-class and out-of-class experiences. Fragmenting the student experience into the "functional silos" of a college or university hinders the maximum potential of student learning and integration of material. This chapter will cover the theories and collaborative pedagogy underlying learning communities, and will provide an overview of common learning community models.

Research and Theory

While not a new approach to education, learning communities have been revived, due in part to recent reports addressing concerns about teaching and learning (Stein, 2004). One of these reports (American Association for Higher Education et al., 1998), presented by the Joint Task Force on Student Learning, outlined ten principles for higher education professionals from both academic and student affairs to improve student learning. Four of the principles outlined in that report are particularly relevant to learning communities:

- Learning is fundamentally about *making and maintaining connections*: biologically through neural networks; mentally among concepts, ideas, and meanings; and experientially through interaction between the mind and the environment, self and others,

18

generality and context, deliberation and action.

- Learning is done by *individuals* who are intrinsically *tied to others as social beings*, interacting as competitors or collaborators, constraining or supporting the learning process, and able to enhance learning through cooperation and sharing.
- Learning is strongly *affected by the educational climate* in which it takes place: the settings and surroundings, the influence of others, and the values accorded to the life of the mind and to learning achievements.
- Much learning *takes place informally and incidentally*, beyond explicit teaching or the classroom, in casual contacts with faculty and staff, peers, campus life, active social and community involvements, and unplanned but fertile and complex situations. (pp. 3, 6–8)

Learning communities promote these principles through the *intentional collaborative restructuring* of the curriculum and the space for learning.

The Learning Paradigm

Learning communities are one example of a reform in learning that fosters student participation to develop knowledge. Robert Barr and John Tagg (1995) describe a paradigm shift in American higher education from the traditional "Instruction Paradigm," where students passively receive knowledge through instruction, to the "Learning Paradigm," where students and instructors are active participants in the acquisition of knowledge. Learning communities both exemplify and benefit from the rise of this constructivist approach to education, whereby knowledge is construed "not as something that is transferred in an authoritarian structure from teacher to student but rather as something that teachers and students work interdependently to develop" (Cross, 1998, p. 5, paraphrasing William Whipple).

Colleges and universities that espouse the Learning Paradigm become learning organizations in which all members of the institution work in partnership to achieve the mission of every college and university: to learn. J. S. Brown (1997) describes five values all learning organizations should espouse:

1. All members of the organization are learners.
2. Learning is natural, healthy, and something that we all seek—making fewer hierarchical distinctions of teachers and learners.
3. Consider the learner as a complex system who is affected by many experiences over a lifetime.
4. Focus on the group of learners, not individual learners, by utilizing

approaches to learning that are powerful for all kinds of learners.
5. Set as the highest priority for institutional strength the designing of structures that require cross-discipline learning. (pp. 8–9)

Learning communities intentionally restructure the curriculum and residential environments in a way consistent with these values.

The Learning Paradigm defines success by focusing on outcomes, specifically student learning outcomes: What have students learned? How much have students learned? Are students able to make connections in their classes across disciplines? How successfully are students able to apply what they have learned to out-of-class scenarios? Answering these questions requires assessment before, throughout, and following the experience. Defining outcomes in this way shifts the focus of the faculty-reward system from the hours faculty members spend teaching a class, grading papers, or holding office hours to the amount of learning students achieve, and to the environ-ments structured by faculty and the methods faculty members create for students to best learn (Barr and Tagg 1995). Learning communities further promote the Learning Paradigm because they focus on student learning outcomes.

Collaborative Learning

Learning communities are also one way to approach collaborative learning, "an umbrella term for a variety of educational approaches involving joint intellectual efforts by students, or students and teachers together" (Smith & MacGregor, 1992, p. 585). Collaborative learning vibrantly illustrates the shift from the Instruction Paradigm to the Learning Paradigm. In such a model, the teacher designs and facilitates activities where the students work in groups to explore the course material. Activities are arranged so students apply the material to tackle problems, generate products, or actively contribute to the conversation in search of conceptual understanding.

Barbara Leigh Smith and Jean MacGregor discuss a number of assumptions that define collaborative learning. First, "learning is an active, constructive process" in which learners assimilate, reorganize, and restructure their understanding of their environments. Conversations are at the heart of collaborative learning, because learning is social and is better accomplished through social interactions with peers and teachers. Learning also depends on activities that challenge students to practice and apply their critical thinking skills. There are, additionally, "affective and subjective dimensions" to learning, because students begin to see themselves as active owners of their own knowledge, not just as passive recipients of textbook and lecture material. Finally, "learners are diverse" (191), and consequently homogeneous teaching methods will not be able to accommodate all learning styles (Smith & MacGregor, 1992, p. 191).

In the late 1990s, the National Center for Teaching, Learning, and Assessment supported Vincent Tinto's study of the coordinated studies programs at Seattle Central Community College (Tinto, 1997). Tinto's results support the pedagogy of learning communities. First, he found that shared classroom experiences in learning communities facilitated relationships between students that extended to out-of-class experiences to a greater extent than was true for non–learning community students. Second, according to Tinto, the combined academic and social involvement of students with their peers enhanced the effort and quality of their contribution to collaborative learning. Third, students perceived the amount and quality of their learning to be greater because of their participation in the learning community. Finally, Tinto's study found that students in learning communities demonstrated greater persistence, involvement, and academic achievement. Tinto provided positive evidence that learning communities and collaborative learning could create a "seamless" learning environment.

Common Learning Community Models

Gabelnick, MacGregor, Matthews, and Smith (1990) were the first to describe learning community models; their models have been redefined and simplified as the learning community movement has progressed (Shapiro & Levine, 1999; Stein, 2004). In all of the learning community models described below, the connections students make between their classes depend heavily on the faculty's resources and efforts to integrate the curriculum. At one end of the spectrum, the amount of faculty investment can be minimal, so that the curriculum and planned activities are loosely tied together, and students benefit socially from having the same peers in multiple classes. On the other, faculty can invest significant effort in integrating their syllabi and activities for maximum student learning. The more intentionally syllabi and activities are coordinated, the more likely it is the learning community will realize the learning outcomes intended (Shapiro & Levine, 1999).

Since learning communities address needs unique to each campus, there is no definitive prescription or best model for learning communities (Shapiro & Levine, 1999). The definitions below, derived from Shapiro and Levine (1999), are flexible, as the needs of colleges and universities vary, but they give a common language to the discussion of learning communities.

Linked

In their simplest form, learning communities that include intentionally structured curricula link two classes together around a theme. Generally, there is a skill course that is linked with a content course, such as a writing course paired with an introductory psychology course. Both classes are reserved for the twenty to thirty students enrolled in the linked learning community. Faculty members involved with linked learning communities are required to invest little time or resources compared to those involved in other learning community models because they must coordinate only their activities and two syllabi.

Clustered

Clustered learning communities expand the linked learning community to three or four courses organized around an interdisciplinary theme. The classes are still reserved for the twenty to thirty students enrolled in the learning community. However, since there are more syllabi to coordinate, the cluster model requires additional effort from participating faculty members. Often instructors will attend one another's classes to better understand their colleagues' material and be more intentional about integrating it into their own courses.

First-Year Interest Group

The first-year interest group (FIG) is the easiest of all the learning communities to create, in terms of its organizational structure and cost of implementation. A FIG is comprised of a small group of students who take a shared seminar class, generally led by an upper-class peer advisor. The students' other classes are comprised of three to four large lecture courses shared with students who are not enrolled in the FIG. In this learning community model, faculty members are not required to work together, change their syllabi, or integrate their material with other disciplines.

In the weekly seminars, the peer advisor helps students make academic connections among their classes. Additionally, peer leaders take time to help first-year students learn about campus resources, acclimate to college, and form study groups. They also provide students with space to discuss frustrations and satisfactions. This model is popular at large research institutions where large lectures are most common.

Coordinated Studies

Coordinated studies programs require the largest investment of resources in terms of faculty time and curriculum integration. Faculty involvement is comprehensive, as it involves establishing the interdisciplinary theme, planning the curriculum, teaching the classes, planning activities outside the classroom, and meeting regularly to discuss course integration and student development.

In this model, a minimum of two academic courses can generate a coordinated learning community, although a student's entire academic schedule can be comprised of the learning community classes. When students and faculty members do not have classes outside of the learning community, extra-curricular experiences such as retreats or field trips are easier to schedule because everyone's class time can be flexible.

Residential and Theme

A residential component can complement any learning community experience. It can also stand alone as its own model of a learning community, sometimes under the name of theme housing. Residence-based learning communities, when connected with courses, create permeable boundaries between in-class and out-of-class learning through collaboration among residence life pro-fessionals and faculty, who work to integrate scholarship into the living environments of their students. Any learning community involving a residen-tial component requires an added effort of partnership between students and academic affairs.

Learning communities established within the residence halls provide a plethora of opportunities for interactions between faculty, staff, and students. Space in the hall, such as lounges, can be used as classrooms, for study or review sessions, for intimate conversations with academic speakers, or for faculty office hours. If space permits, faculty members can have their offices located in the residence hall, too.

Alexander Astin has defined student involvement as "the amount of physical and psychological energy that the student devotes to the academic experience" (Astin, 1993, p. 297). The student involvement theory defines student achievement as a direct function of the time and effort students commit to activities designed to produce student success. From this standpoint, it is rational to conclude that students in a residential learning community, in which they focus on an academic or social issue in their classes in their residence hall and participate in other activities supporting the learning community, will have larger learning gains.

Peer Mentors

Peer mentors can assist in curriculum integration and activities in any learning community model. Peers may be able to help students develop and learn more than faculty or staff, insofar as the peer group is "the single most important environmental influence on student development" (Astin, 1993, p. xiv). Astin suggests that the intentional use of peer groups positively influences the development and learning of students. Steven Ender and Fred Newton (2000) emphasize the value of paraprofessionals as models: "There are very positive benefits attained by observation of the action of another person who has gone through similar changes and experiences" (p. 7). Peer mentors can participate in learning communities by advising, tutoring, instructing, modeling roles, or facilitating conversations formally and informally.

Conclusion

Creating learning communities requires resources, time to plan and collaborate, and commitment from staff, faculty, and students. Learning communities compel professionals to think about learning in different ways, and encourage the construction of environments that maximize learning outcomes. Thus, they are not a "quick fix" to the ills of higher education. Forming learning communities requires creating learning objectives, planning assessments, coordinating syllabi, arranging spaces in residence halls, and educating stakeholders about learning communities. The benefits of learning communities, however, usually outweigh the costs of the time and resources required. Students achieve stronger learning outcomes, cross-disciplinary learning, and connections with faculty and staff (Stassen, 2003; Zhao & Kuh, 2004). Overall, the purposeful arrangements of learning communities help facilitate a better undergraduate experience.

References

American Association for Higher Education, American College Personnel Association, & National Association of Student Personnel Administrators. (1998). *Powerful partnerships: A shared responsibility of learning.* Washington, DC: Authors.

Astin, A. W. (1993). *What matters in college: Four critical years revisited.* San Francisco: Jossey-Bass.

Barr, R. B., & Tagg, J. (1995). From teaching to learning: A new paradigm for undergraduate education. *Change, 27*(6), 154–166.

Brown, J. S. (1997). On becoming a learning organization. *About Campus, 1* (6), 5–10.

Cross, K. P. (1998). Why learning communities? Why now? *About Campus, 3* (3), 4–11.

Ender, S. C., & Newton, F. B. (2000). *Students helping students: A guide for peer educators on college campuses.* San Francisco: Jossey-Bass.

Gabelnick, F., MacGregor, J., Matthews, R. S., & Smith, B. L. (1990). *Learning communities: Creating connections among students, faculty, and disciplines.* New Directions for Teaching and Learning, 41. San Francisco: Jossey-Bass.

Kuh, G. D. (1996). Guiding principles for creating seamless learning environments for undergraduates. *Journal of College Student Development, 37*(2), 135–148.

Shapiro, N. S., & Levine, J. H. (1999). *Creating learning communities.* San Francisco: Jossey-Bass.

Smith, B. L., & MacGregor, J. T. (1992). What is collaborative learning? In A. S. Goodsell, M. Maher, V. Tinto, B. L. Smith, & J. MacGregor (Eds.), *Collaborative learning: A sourcebook for higher education* (pp. 585–586). University Park, PA: National Center on Postsecondary Teaching, Learning, and Assessment.

Stassen, M. (2003). Student outcomes: The impact of varying living-learning community models. *Research in Higher Education, 44*(5), 581–613.

Stein, R. F. (2004). Learning communities: An overview. In S. N. Hurd & F. S. Stein (Eds.), *Building and Sustaining Learning Communities: The Syracuse University Experience* (pp. 1–18). Bolton, MA: Anker.

Tinto, V. (1997). Classrooms as communities: Exploring the educational character of student persistence. *Journal of Higher Education, 68*(6), 599–623.

Zhao, C.-M., & Kuh, G. D. (2004). Adding value: Learning communities and student engagement. *Research in Higher Education, 45*(2), 115–138.

Tips and Strategies for Assessing Learning Communities

Jared Halter and Camila Lértora Nardozzi

"LABORATORY in Learning Communities" is a unique course that is offered as part of the higher education master's program at Syracuse University. As graduate students, we took part in the course, which focused on current types of learning communities as well as the history of the practice, models for successful development, and techniques for assessment. The course required that we observe participants of several first-year learning communities at Syracuse University, Le Moyne College, and SUNY College of Environmental Science and Forestry. These observations included classes, learning community retreats, and learning community planning meetings with the respective faculty and staff.

At the end of the semester, after we had integrated ourselves into the lives of these various learning communities, we were asked to complete an assessment of one community to help us further understand the experiences of students. We broke into groups of two or three with the purpose of conducting focus groups comprised of five to ten students from each learning community. We prepared by developing lists of questions based on the main theme of our study, how participating in learning communities contributed to students' learning. Our questions involved a range of topics, such as the importance of course connections, faculty–student relationships, peer-to-peer relationships, out-of-class activities, living arrangements, and diversity within the learning community and at the institution as a whole. Throughout this process we kept in mind that the answers to these questions were from the particular student's perspective and were not representative of every member of the learning community.

The course, our experiences, and what we learned throughout the assessment process provided us with insight into the importance of formal assessment for the success of learning communities. We also developed strategies that we hope will help others who might plan to work with learning communities and conduct assessments in the future.

The Assessment Process

As Nancy J. Evans, Deanna S. Forney, and Florence Guido-DiBrito (1998) suggest, "assessment and evaluation must be a part of every intentionally designed developmental intervention. Interventions must be intentionally planned and based on sound assessment data reflecting the needs of the student community" (p. 289). Assessments are a means for improving programs, meeting goals, and obtaining informative and useful learning outcomes. For present purposes, we define assessment as "the systematic and ongoing method of gathering, analyzing and using information from measured outcomes to improve student learning" (Selim & Pet-Armacost, 2004, p. 2).

From our experience, the knowledge gained through assessment proved invaluable to administrators and faculty involved in the planning and implementation of learning communities and their activities. This process helped identify and measure many factors essential for improvement of the programs. Some of the components positively impacted by the performance of assessment were idea creation and expansion, strengths and weaknesses, program effectiveness, individual facilitator performance, learning outcomes, and goal achievement (Selim & Pet-Armacost, 2004).

Some involved with learning communities might argue they can personally identify and measure the aforementioned parts of the program without formal assessment. While we would not deny this possibility, we have found formal assessment results are essential in supporting informal observations and hypotheses, providing knowledge and insight beyond informal observation, and creating deeper and more meaningful understanding. Also, the importance of hearing the voices behind the experiences cannot be diminished. The stories shared by students proved invaluable for us in understanding what it meant to be involved in their particular learning community, what did and did not work, why it did or did not work, what issues needed to be reconsidered, and what elements should be continued and further developed.

The Conceptual Framework of Assessment

During our semester in "Laboratory in Learning Communities," we came to appreciate that one of the most important aspects of assessment is understanding and following a well-laid-out plan. Assessors must decide which research method to use (qualitative or quantitative) and how they will use the results for improvement and change. Susan Jones (2002) outlines seven steps that we found useful in developing and designing an effective assessment plan: (1) method selection, (2) tool design, (3) assessment performance, (4) data gathering and compilation, (5) analysis of findings, (6) report production, and (7) implementation of results.

Method Selection and Tool Design

"Method refers to the actual techniques used to gather data and analyze results (e.g., individual interviews, focus groups)" (Jones, 2002, p. 469). In this step, the desired assessment technique is decided: qualitative, quantitative, or a combination of the two. In choosing a method, assessors must distinguish the type of findings desired and decide how these findings will be utilized.

The method selected determines how the assessment is executed. After the appropriate method has been chosen, assessors should take extreme care in designing the proper assessment tool. Generally, questionnaires or surveys are used for quantitative assessments, and interviews or focus groups are used for qualitative assessments. Once an initial draft of the assessment tool is designed, revisions should be made.

For the purpose of our learning community assessment, our professor asked us to conduct focus groups with the participants of the various learning communities that we had integrated ourselves into. Conducting focus groups was a great way to get the students' input on their experiences as learning community participants; we could ask students to flesh out their ideas through detailed and specific questions during these focus groups. A quantitative study (such as a Likert-scale survey) would not have afforded the same opportunity.

Assessment Performance

In this part of the process, the actual assessment plan is put to practice. Some might consider assessment performance the most important part of assessment, but we disagree. Although we do understand this step is significant, we believe each step is equally valuable and essential to the process.

One thing to note is the importance of confidentiality and the anonymity of participants and the information they provide during assessment. The participants need to know the information they are being asked to give will remain anonymous, so they feel safe in being honest and open. In order to preserve the confidentiality and anonymity of participants when preparing our final assessment report for the Learning Community Team (faculty and staff), we asked each participant to choose a pseudonym, by which they would refer to themselves throughout the focus groups. In order to distinguish who was speaking, we asked each participant to announce him or herself (for example, "This is Carol speaking") every time he/she spoke. We then used these pseudonyms in the final report when referring to specific comments made by participants. In facilitating an interview or focus group, such as we did, it is important to ensure that participants grant permission to the researchers to use their experiences in the final assessment report by signing consent forms. For quantitative assessments, surveys and questionnaires should be submitted anonymously.

Data Gathering and Compilation

After performing the assessment, thorough analysis demands sorting the data and compiling it into groups and categories. Although this step may be tedious and time consuming, it is necessary for successful assessment. Interviews or focus group discussions should be tape-recorded and then transcribed so assessors can code them by themes, which helps in writing the final report. Recording the interview or focus group process is essential in creating a thorough and accurate assessment report. Robert Bogdan and Sari Biklen (1998) write about implications for the researcher–subject relationship when recording the session:

> If you choose to use a tape recorder, ask respondents if they mind. The point in the encounter where you ask permission can be touchy. Either out of shyness or out of fear of being turned down, many have a difficult time raising the issue. Never record without permission. Force yourself to ask.... The tape recorder should be thought of as a third party that cannot see. When subjects gesture or show size with their hands, these nonverbal cues have to be translated into verbal language so that the tape recorder can play them back for typing. (pp. 100–101)

Analyzing, Reporting, and Implementing Findings

Once the data from the focus group is gathered, compiled, and sorted, it is time to put inductive and deductive skills to use for thorough analysis. Identifying participants (pseudonymously, as described above) when analyzing data, trends, and common themes will provide greater insight into the experiences of a learning community and will help to organize the data in a way that will be useful when producing the final assessment report. This report should be a summary of findings from the focus groups conducted, and should include recommendations supported by the collected data and supplemented by professional literature when applicable. Once this report is produced, we recommend you meet with those involved in the study to discuss the findings. These meetings should be purposefully and intentionally focused on preparing an action plan that is grounded in concrete data and relevant literature support.

Challenges and Strategies of Assessment

We encountered many challenges in our experience of developing and conducting focus groups for assessment. The strategies we present here grew from those challenges.

During our assessment, we briefly described the focus-group process to the learning community students, asked them to sign consent forms, and began reading our scripted introduction and guidelines (for many of us, these focus groups were our first assessment experience, so having scripted introductions, guidelines, and questions turned out to be of utmost value). Formal introductions and explanations are important to getting a focus group off to a good start. During this step, assessors should review the purpose of the study, the guidelines for discussion, issues of confidentiality and anonymity, how the information collected will be used, and the importance of using pseudonyms to protect the participants' identities in the final assessment report (Morgan, 1997).

Questions in any type of qualitative study, such as a focus group, should follow some general guidelines. First, assessors should start with questions they feel interviewees will be comfortable in answering. This helps create a rapport or level of trust between the facilitator and participants. In our focus group, we asked questions about the students' relationships with each other and about whether their living arrangements helped create a feeling of "community" for them. One should strive to keep questions open-ended (e.g., "How did you feel about taking classes with the people you live with?"). Closed questions (e.g., "Did you find it difficult to live and take classes with the same people?") may be leading, and could be perceived as imposing words and feelings on the participants.

While questions in a qualitative study should be cohesive, it is also acceptable to ask questions that might spontaneously arise out of the participants' responses. In our group, for example, some participants discussed the differences between the two sections of the learning community, allowing us to follow up with unplanned questions about the dynamic between the two sections. As Elizabeth Whitt writes, "An initial set of questions should be developed to provide direction for the interviews, although the interviews should not be so structured that fruitful areas of information about which you are unaware are missed" (1993, p. 84). Also, facilitators should probe and push as much as possible (without making participants feel uncomfortable) to mine valuable information for the assessment of the learning community. Since focus groups generally consist of five to eight participants, facilitators should draft no more than eight to ten questions, and should anticipate asking only six or seven of them during the hour or 90 minutes that the focus group should last.

While drafting questions, conducting the focus group, and putting together our assessment of the learning community, we learned many strategies for future assessments, some of them through trial and error. One particular challenge involved building a rapport with students involved in the focus group, so they felt comfortable enough to share their personal experiences with us. It was difficult to get the students to talk freely within the group, and just as difficult to make sure that everyone got a chance to speak, without allowing one person to dominate the conversation (Bogdan & Biklen, 1998). We also had to strive to get a feel for the central theme of what was being discussed. This could be complicated at times, as when the students contradicted one another or themselves (for instance, one student discussed the advantages of living and taking classes together, while also complaining about not getting to meet other students on campus because she was always with her learning community peers). Other challenges involved reframing questions in order to elicit a response from the students (e.g., "How did the out-of-class activities supplement the overall theme of the learning community?" vs. "Tell me about how the out-of-class experiences contributed to your learning") and recognizing and compensating for having prematurely reached conclusions about the students' experiences after speaking with them only once in the focus group.

Before we conducted our focus groups, we learned some techniques that help participants feel comfortable speaking openly with us. We found it was imperative to maintain eye contact with the students since we were asking them to release personal information. We also adopted a suggestion that we refrain from taking notes while listening to responses; this can create a feeling of nervousness in the participants, which might discourage them from being as open during the focus group as they otherwise would. Writing notes during a focus group can also be distracting for both the participants and the assessors. Some level of formality, however, should be maintained. The assessor's rapport with the participants should be professional, but not so professional that the participants are intimidated or uncomfortable. It is important to balance a welcoming, comfortable atmosphere with an atmosphere of professionalism.

Perhaps the biggest challenge we met while conducting assessment through a qualitative study was always reminding ourselves that the responses given by the participants/interviewees were subjective; these responses were based on the students' perceptions of *their own* experiences in being in a learning community. It was important to keep in mind that, for the most part, the participating students had not had an opportunity to reflect upon their internal development in the community. Typically, first-year students are not ready to comprehend that college is indeed an ongoing developmental process in their identity formation (Chickering, 1969). Students therefore are unlikely to recognize, or perhaps appreciate, the knowledge they have received from being part of a learning community and interacting with peers and faculty. Nor are they likely to appreciate the learning community's contribution to their identity development. So, when writing the final assessment report, assessors should always keep in mind that answers come through the lens of a student's perception of his or her experience and may not reflect the perceptions of the entire group.

Conclusion

Assessing a learning community is not quick or easy. What we have gained from our experience is a series of necessary and valuable strategies and steps for performing future assessments. Whether members of the academic community work in academic affairs or student affairs, the ability to conduct assessments is an essential skill. All of us will eventually encounter situations in which we must assess the performance of individuals, an office, a department, or a group such as a learning community. We hope our experiences and the steps and tips we have provided will help to make those assessments more successful.

References

Bogdan, R. C., & Biklen, S. K. (1998). *Qualitative research for education: An introduction to theory and methods* (3rd ed.). Needham Heights, MA: Allyn and Bacon.

Chickering, A. W. (1969). *Education and identity.* San Francisco: Jossey-Bass.

Evans, N., Forney, D., & Guido-DiBrito, F. (1998). Future directions for theory in student development practice. In *Student development in college: Theory, research, and practice* (pp. 280–291). San Francisco: Jossey-Bass.

Jones, S. (2002). (Re)Writing the word: Methodological strategies and issues in qualitative research. *Journal of College Student Development, 43*, 461–473.

Morgan, D. L. (1997). *Focus groups as qualitative research.* Thousand Oaks, CA: Sage.

Selim, B. R., & Pet-Armacost, J. (2004). *Program assessment handbook: Guidelines for planning and implementing quality enhancing efforts of program and student learning outcomes.* Orlando: University of Central Florida.

Whitt, E. (1993). Making the familiar strange: Discovering culture. In G. Kuh (Ed.), *Cultural Perspectives in Student Affairs Work* (pp. 81–94). Lanham, MD: University Press of America.

Learning Communities Assessment
Challenges and Recommendations from Faculty and Staff Perspectives

W. Leslie Burleson and Michele Tarnow

WHILE one learning community thrives on the campus of Syracuse University, another has trouble getting its members to participate in planned events. Some communities require participants to take three-credit courses; others require no coursework. Experience among learning community leaders varies from five years to none at all. Though the learning communities at Syracuse University are based on the same general concept, each operates differently within its own structure. A qualitative assessment conducted during the 2005–2006 academic year set out to determine what the leaders of these learning communities can learn from each other and how their differences affect their levels of success. The result is a list of recommendations that should improve the quality of the learning community experiences for students across all interests and departments.

Methods

For five months during the 2005–2006 academic year, interviews were conducted across 12 learning communities. The goal was to understand, among other things, what challenges faced learning community team members and to formulate recommendations for improving all learning communities across the university. Interviews totaled 19 in all (8 faculty, 6 staff, and 5 joint faculty/ staff). Exactly one-half of the learning communities included in the study were within their first year of operation. Conversely, the remaining one-half had been in existence since the 1999–2000 academic year. All participating learning communities were located within residence halls. Nine of the learning communities required that students take one or more courses; three had no courses formally linked to them.

The purpose of the interviews was to learn more about faculty and staff experiences working with learning communities. Separate protocols were developed for faculty interviews and staff interviews. These were designed to remain fluid and were frequently updated during data collection to serve as guides that informed the interview process rather than as stringent data-collection tools.

The findings of this study are presented in three sections: faculty challenges, staff challenges, and recommendations. Details are provided in the form of general themes. Representative samples of faculty and staff comments are also included where appropriate. These results are part of a larger assessment of the university's learning communities. As a result, some recommendations presented here include responses to the findings listed below and to themes that emerged as part of the overall assessment.

Faculty Challenges

Faculty members interviewed had been involved with their particular learning communities for varying amounts of time, ranging from one to five years. Regardless, the study found that all faculty faced similar challenges.

Course Issues

Some faculty found it important to have a regular course associated with learning communities. One faculty member emphasized this: "If we want learning communities to be something that's recognized across campus ... [there] needs to be a three-credit class."

Members of one new learning community that had no associated class expressed difficulty attracting students to participate in planned events. They blamed this lack of participation, in part, on the lack of a required class. "As too many students are not invested or involved," one member said, "it would work better if [the learning community] were connected with a class."

Student Behavior in Classes/Course Management Issues

One concern that emerged from faculty interviews was that students who are part of learning communities become too familiar with each other because they live on the same floor and are constantly interacting with each other. As one faculty member put it, "There's something that can translate into insufficient seriousness regarding the nature of the classroom experience because of the ease that is induced by being with your buddies."

Another faculty member shared this experience:

We had a few problems a couple of years ago with a kind of hyper-bonding with the guys on the floor, and I think it gets to a point where these students are so tightly put together in the academic area and in the residential area that there are some that have had enough, and they need a little more space, and so I would say that is kind of a challenge at times.

Coordination with Other Instructors

Several learning communities attributed their success to the regular meetings held throughout the semester. For example, in one learning community the instructors met for lunch each week. This extra level of communication enabled them to tie portions of their classes together. "I can get some of her stuff into my class, and she can get some of my stuff into her class," one instructor said. Another faculty member expressed similar feelings:

> We meet once a week as a group to kind of figure out what's going on with everybody. It's kind of the key to how this works. I think that's why our learning community works well.... I mean, they are time consuming but we couldn't give them up.... You need to know what each other is doing and sometimes you find yourself just modifying a little bit of what you've got planned because of how it can fit with something else going on that particular week.

Staff Challenges

Approximately one-third of the staff interviewed for this study had been working with one or more learning communities for three or more years. The remaining two-thirds of the staff interviewees were participating with learning communities for the first time. Like their faculty counterparts, staff members discussed a number of challenges they experienced during their participation in their learning communities.

Student Participation

Staff expressed concern about a lack of, or waning participation of, students in the smaller and newer learning communities. If membership numbers are too small, they said, it can be difficult to get a reliable contingent to show up for activities to make the events meaningful. As one frustrated staff member said, "I didn't consider that would be a problem. So, it was more, what are we going to do, how do we arrange these activities? So, when they just started not showing up for events it was frustrating and I wasn't quite sure how to do it."

Non-linked Courses

Learning communities that do not have linked courses tend to have the hardest time maintaining high levels of participation, according to staff members. One staff member said, "I do think if it was associated with a class, that would be a big improvement because they'd be more invested in it and there'd be a better relationship formed between the students and the instructor."

Another staff member expressed similar feelings. "It's not a class; I can't hold it over them. They're all busy. They have other extracurricular activities. They're taking full course loads. That was, for me, a bit of an issue."

Competition for Student Involvement

Mandatory student attendance at other campus events can also create problems. One staff member remarked that

> this university grossly overloads freshmen with things they have to do, things they have to attend, mandatory this, mandatory that.... So, if you've got a cool learning community with stuff going on, you're competing for a very scarce amount of student time, and it gets frustrating, especially when you've invested as much as we've invested with staff.

Another staff member shared,

> We just didn't leave enough room and space for these kids to be freshmen in any possible way that word can be applied. They have literally hundreds of new experiences, hundreds of new opportunities, all this freedom. For most of them, it's a much harder workload than they have been used to in high school ... so we really cut down, substantially, the amount of programming in the first semester.

Faculty Commitment and Team Incentives

Some staff members indicated they had difficulty generating and maintaining faculty interest, given that working with learning communities is extra work for faculty who already carry full loads of coursework and research concerns. One faculty member agreed this is a problem: "To do the job as well as I would like to do it, it's probably 30 to 35 hours per week; right now I spend 18 to 20. I spend 65 hours minimum teaching the three classes that I teach. Sometimes one or the other suffers, because of one or the other."

The use of incentives was suggested as a means of motivating team members to participate. One staff member reported that "it doesn't have to be that much of a reward, but just something that recognizes who were the team players that year, and what did they do to make that a big success? That would, I think, help in two ways: number one, you would reward a team for doing something good; [number two], you also would put it in the forefront; what did they do and how can other teams model theirs after a successful program?"

Recommendations

Faculty and staff members offered a number of recommendations they believed would enhance their learning communities. Most of these were administrative in nature and were made by both faculty and staff members.

1) Link a three-credit course to all learning communities. Linkage to a three-credit course taught by a faculty member (rather than a staff member) bolsters the credibility of learning communities. Members of one learning community team revealed that they see

> a general need out there to have the academy buy in and say "these are valid courses that need to have an arts and sciences moniker to them," so, I think that's a huge issue; if somebody could say to us in the fall, we're going to give you a three-credit course that's going to be formalized, there are loads of things that we could do. But why should we put any more motivation or energy into a one-credit class when, after this fall, it may not exist again? And I think it won't happen unless we have some kind of a faculty liaison.

2) Understand the impact of student "hyper-bonding" and its potential for creating behavioral challenges in and out of the classroom. Recognize that students may "need a little more space" and incorporate learning exercises that also nurture individual thinking and creativity.

3) Encourage regularly scheduled meetings among all learning community team members to promote communication among faculty as well as between faculty and staff members. As one staff member indicated, the success of their learning community was a result of their collaboration with faculty. "Something as simple as having that individual time with the faculty member, [is what] I really think makes a learning community work. Otherwise, it's no different than any other floor that I have in the building."

4) Provide collaborative information-sharing opportunities among learning communities. Although faculty members expressed satisfaction with the support from the Office of Learning Communities, it was suggested that an additional opportunity to collaborate would prove helpful. One faculty member said,

> We all kind of interact autonomously. We've all got our one formula.... There's no opportunity to sit down in a general forum and say, "these are the best things and the results of your assessment would be great if they're shared with all of us," because I'm sure there are great successes going on in other learning communities, but we have no clue.

5) Target a minimum number of students essential for a successful learning community experience. The impact of other demands on students' time management leads to waning activity participation. A staff member relayed the following example: "One of my learning communities has 28 [students] and we have regular attendance of 15 to 16 people. [When] ten people are missing, it still looks like there's that larger presence."

6) Continue to recruit resident advisors from existing pool of learning community participants. One faculty member indicated that these advisors understand what the students are experiencing and are able to be supportive of first-year experiences. "I would want that to be kind of an insurance that we definitely find a good [student in the department] who wants to do the RA position as well. I think that that has really banked on the success of it."

7) Provide incentives (e.g., recognition, rewards) to learning community team members for their participation. Incentives for staff as well as faculty in the form of recognition and rewards were recommended as a means of showcasing the success of individual learning communities and increasing the commitment of team members to their communities.

PART TWO

TEACHING AND LEARNING
IN A LEARNING COMMUNITY

The Arts Adventure LC
A Classroom-to-Community Cultural Connection

Eileen Strempel

WHEN I agreed to participate in the Arts Adventure Learning Community at Syracuse University, I was thrilled by the prospect of reaching new students and eager to become part of the program. I had no idea, however, what a dramatic impact the students and the experience would have on my own professional development and on my relationship with the university community as a whole.

Syracuse University's Arts Adventure Learning Community was founded in the fall of 2001 by Martha Sutter, dean of students in the College of Visual and Performing Arts, in response to a request by our vice-chancellor at the time, Deborah Freund. However, the original learning community (LC) did not have a required course to provide critical focus and structure. Thus, the next spring I was approached about incorporating my course as the core class for the LC.

I believed Fine Arts (FIA) 195: Performance Live would be ideal for an LC entitled "Arts Adventure." Central to this course is a learning environment in which students are exposed to performing musicians and their music. Live performances reach students in an immediate and visceral way. The performances draw on many different types of performance traditions—including non-Western and Western as well as classical and popular music—to promote wide-ranging appreciation. Music has diverse social functions in various cultures around the globe; the material encourages students to think and write about music from cross-cultural perspectives. Ideally, this broader vantage point ultimately provokes a thoughtful re-examination of one's own music and culture. However, in order to attain these course objectives, students need to master not only basic theoretical principles of music, but also a vocabulary with which to discuss musical sound. A central demand of the course was that students write clearly, reflectively, and critically about their musical experiences. Ironically, it was this writing challenge that later cemented my relationship to the LCs.

This was my first LC experience and I was unsure what to expect. One immediate "plus" was that students strolled into class together, already talking with their new friends about the course material. I loved this vibrant classroom energy. However, as the semester progressed, several challenges became clear. I was frustrated by the perceived sense of anonymity in my enlarged class and, furthermore, I was concerned with the quality of student writing. Seeking assistance, I consulted the Syracuse University Writing Center. I discovered warm and experienced staff members, and they offered numerous helpful suggestions. After several planning meetings, a team of instructors entered my class. Each leader facilitated an intimate writing circle focused on a recently shared musical performance. I recognized the increased dialogue and discussion afforded by the smaller groups and, to my delight, the quality of student papers noticeably improved after this isolated exercise.

Out of this experience, I became intrigued by the possibilities of sustained collaboration with the writing program. (Perhaps this was merely selfish, as the improved papers made for more enjoyable reading and grading.) It was clear that the timing of any intervention was critical; for the greatest benefit any link should be initiated at the start of the student's first year, from the outset of the first class. As I mulled over the challenges and possibilities, one of the writing facilitators began a conversation with me.

This writing center specialist was a veteran professor in the writing program, Steve Thorley. Sensing kindred spirits in one another, we began plotting how we might work together to refine and expand our limited classroom experiment. He had noticed in writing sections offered for students in the College of Visual and Performing Arts that undergraduates interested in and experienced with the arts brought with them a better understanding of the creative process than the typical non-arts student. This understanding enabled him to forge connections between the making of writing and the making of music and art. He suggested building on their familiarity and experience with the process. As we conversed, we formed the concept of linking the first-year writing course (Writing 105) with both Performance Live and the Arts Adventure LC.

Thus, one of the highlights of my college teaching career began in the fall of 2003 as the link between and among students, faculty, and performing artists formed a true learning community. As teachers, we found that we could harness student enthusiasm for the subject matter in order to motivate students to engage in serious inquiry. Steve and I both independently chose to move students from purely personal reflection to a broader, more audience-focused orientation; Steve noted that, as a result, "students in both courses repeatedly practiced and honed key skills involved in writing about music—sonic description, description of cultural context, interpretation of what music 'is' and 'does' and 'means' in a culture"—all of which was encouraged by two professors fostering cross-course dialogue. Our students came to realize that personal experience and "taste" are embedded in and connected to larger issues of culture.

This approach showed clear benefits. In both courses students progressed from initial "personal" activities to essays that wrestled with rather than retreated from complexity, with writing that was richly descriptive. A cursory glance at my Excel Gradebook revealed this quality difference in the course grades as well. Students in the LC earned grades that were nine percent higher than those outside of the LC, a significant improvement that could make a huge difference in GPAs. The only noteworthy difficulty was an increase in plagiarism. Living in close proximity with each other apparently encouraged a "group project" approach toward individual homework assignments. I was not prepared for the increase in papers containing a high degree of similarity in content and syntax. I found that taking class time to read and discuss the university plagiarism policy (now included in my syllabus) helped to alleviate the situation. My subsequent reframing of the assignments to include more personal reflection also served to prevent plagiarism from the outset.

The performances at the center of the assignments in both classes not only served as a shared vehicle for instruction, but also provided connective social experiences for those in the LC. Outside of the classroom and on the auditorium floor, Steve and I would meet, discuss our teaching and students, and speculate on the upcoming (or ongoing) concert. Our visible modeling of intellectual inquiry and curiosity often encouraged a circle of students to "check in" with us, edging closer to eavesdrop on or participate in our conversation. The animated, lively and informal discussions that the students witnessed on the part of their professors had more impact than any classroom lecture. Seeing teachers not only as human beings but also as friends further consolidated the sense of community.

The connection between curricular and co-curricular activities creates a seamlessly integrated learning environment, an atmosphere that fosters continual dialogue where learning is deepened, enriched, and nuanced. Whether this dialogue consists of informal conversations that that take place in residence halls (that return to a point made in a classroom lecture heard earlier that day) or whether it is the more formal exchanges of the classroom, one is continually urged to link and connect, return and remember. An additional advantage is that students tend to look out for one another more, wondering out loud why someone is not in class and calling (or text messaging) the missing student in order to keep the group together. This sense of genuine concern further impacts the level of dialogue inside and outside of the classroom. Students remind each other of upcoming project due dates or impending exams; this positively impacts the caliber of the work submitted in our classes while reinforcing connections among the students. The LC was so unexpectedly successful that students banded together and petitioned the Residence Life staff for permission to continue living together for their sophomore year. Thus, the Arts Adventure II LC was born.

As we continued with our two linked courses in 2007, both Steve and I continued to grow professionally through the LC connection. Working as part of a team with other faculty members has reinspired and reinvigorated my own teaching. Through this community (and LC retreats) I've met an entire group of faculty that I might never have interacted with otherwise. As an added enhancement, most of these other faculty and staff are the folks who care most about the university. Bringing us together creates awareness of the benefits (and responsibilities) of being a member of an intellectual institution. I have borrowed some of my best teaching ideas from this group of committed educators. We continue to discuss how we might improve our collaboration, and are currently considering a continuation that would link Writing 205 and The History of American Song. This faculty collaboration is critical, and locating a colleague with openness to the LC approach is the key. One might conceive of the process as akin to "distance team teaching" in that, although we don't share the physical space of the same classroom, we do—in the broadest sense—alternate lectures. Although commitment to the LC is usually made for an academic year, finding a complimentary intellectual companion on this journey is a crucial decision, and I would encourage faculty to sign on to the LC with their initial academic partnership already settled.

Through my work in the Arts Adventure LC, I have learned that the LC structure benefits the students in tangible as well as intangible ways. Equally significant, the LC serves as a wellspring for faculty engagement, invigoration, and enjoyment. The result for the university is a rigorous learning environment that manages to simultaneously foster personal connection and academic enrichment.

Creating a Unique Learning Community Through Creativity, Innovation, and Entrepreneurship

Eric M. Alderman

WHEN given the opportunity to start a new learning community at Syracuse University (SU)—a national leader in residence-based learning communities— we envisioned a platform for enhancing students' social and intellectual growth within an environment of university-wide innovation and entrepreneurship. Our vision became reality in the fall of 2004 when the Barbara Glazer Weinstein and Jerome S. Glazer Creativity, Innovation, and Entrepreneurship Learning Community (CIE LC) was launched.[1]

The focus of the CIE LC is to create in its students a vision of themselves as agents of change in the arts and sciences, in commercial and social activities, and in technology. The CIE LC has accomplished this by creating an environment for, and a sustainable model of, student immersion in creative and entrepreneurial endeavors through collaborations, experiences, and the channeling of entrepreneurial potential into all facets of their lives and their greater community.

Creating the Environment

In order to implement an environment permeated by creativity, it was essential to connect a facility, a program, and a student membership unique to the SU campus. The first step was to transform the Dellplain Hall CIE LC Floor into an extraordinary facility. This environment was achieved by underwriting the following physical enhancements:

---

[1] This learning community is an endowed learning community; funds from the endowment are used to support educational programming in the CIE LC.

- cosmetic changes such as new CIE LC logo carpeting, entrance enhancements of wood paneling, and unusual paint colors throughout;
- the creation of an on-floor class and presentation room with state-of-the-art audio-visual capabilities (computer-driven, digital projection, plasma TV, surround sound, etc.);
- the creation of an in-house, on-floor resource lab with twelve modern work stations, each containing media-oriented monitors and full-capability, state-of-the-art creativity hardware and software (both Microsoft- and Mac-based), along with high-speed, high-capability color laser printers and a presentation LCD wall monitor;
- infrastructure improvements to wiring, cable, electrical lines, communications, and HVAC to support the classroom and the resource lab.

Sustainability

Sustainability has been built into the CIE LC model through increasing inclusion of the entrepreneurial program in the CIE LC students' lives as they travel through their university careers. The model is unique in its expectation that CIE LC students will be residential members for two years and non-residential members and upper-class mentors throughout the remainder of their academic programs. The CIE LC goal is to encourage each student to live an entrepreneurial life—to become a dreamer and a doer.

Finding the Students

The initial class of 78 CIE LC residents was culled from a pool of more than 120 applicants, representing six of the nine undergraduate schools and colleges of SU.[2] Initial interest in the CIE LC was generated through a brochure, proactive networking with those at SU who would come in contact with incoming and matriculating students, and an active faculty presence at spring receptions, which are attended by a large number of admitted students prior to their making residential living choices for the next year. Akin to "buzz marketing," each of these interactions kept the CIE LC in the forefront for incoming students and showed a positive energy and commitment that helped others to become as excited about and involved in the CIE LC as its originators. This energy was naturally transferred on a number of levels to the applying and matriculating students as they interacted with SU in their

---

[2] These are the College of Arts and Sciences, the S.I. Newhouse School of Public Communications, the Whitman School of Management, the L.C. Smith College of Engineering and Computer Science, the School of Information Studies, and the College of Human Ecology.

university and housing choice process.

In its first year, the CIE LC had no control over who was accepted into the learning community; enrollment requests for the CIE LC were filled on the same first-come, first-served basis used for all of SU's learning communities. The CIE LC, as a learning community that has an unusual level of programming and demands a high level of time commitment, discovered through this experience that the success of the LC requires that students have a strong desire to participate and the commitment necessary to take advantage of the program content. As a result, in the 2006–2007 academic year, the CIE LC became the first learning community at Syracuse University with its own application process in addition to the learning community enrollment request on the housing application provided to each admitted student.

The Initial Challenge

The initial challenge in creating the CIE LC was the lack of a budget sufficient to support the necessary residence hall renovations. The first order of business was to research and access sources of funding and in-kind gifts. An intense four-month period over the summer prior to opening was used, on the one hand, to make contacts and pursue leads sought through alumni relations, existing corporate sponsorship of SU programs, and national inquiries, and, on the other hand, to find matches with companies whose products, services, and philosophy would support this type of strategic partnership. Ultimately, the budget goal was accomplished through a package of financial and other support from third parties as well as the nationally recognized Entrepreneurship and Emerging Enterprises Department of SU's Whitman School of Management, the SU Department of Computer and Media Services, the SU Office of Design and Construction, and the Chancellor's Office at SU. The Coleman Foundation also provided a generous grant. In all, more than $215,000 was raised, including in-kind gifts from such sources as Intel, Microsoft, Okidata (printers), Motion Computing (tablet PCs) and Seneca Data (a national hardware manufacturer located in the Syracuse area).

The Program

Students in the CIE LC actively participate in a systematic portfolio of programs and are evaluated based on their contributions and performance. Highlights of the program include a complimentary brain-functioning evaluation conducted in the first two weeks using the Hermann Brain Dominance Instrument, the substantive program detailed below, individual achievement awards, and the D'Aniella trophy given at the end of each semester to the highest achieving student team. These awards are made on the basis both of qualitative categories such as creativity, actual innovations, leadership, and the production of assigned deliverables, and of quantitative information in terms of participation.

The programming and recognition are designed to further the important goal of making the residence hall an incubator for thought and action. Below is a sampling of elements that are built into the programming for a given semester.

The CIE LC Course (EEE 110/PAF 200: Discovering the Innovator Within)

Worth one credit per semester and required for two semesters (cross-listed with the Whitman School of Management and the Public Affairs Department in the Maxwell School of Citizenship and Public Affairs), this course is taught in the CIE LC residence hall classroom, using a combination of lecture, interactive exercises, and experiential learning. Students are assigned to teams called Prides and focus on creativity in generating ideas and innovation in the proposed implementation of those ideas.

The initial pedagogy of this course involved a combination of both lecture and participation. However, during the first year, instructors observed that the multiple demands of a first-year student's life, with its new opportunities in a university setting, created an adverse dynamic for the students. When comparing the relative importance of this one-credit course with the required courses within each student's major and the desire to sample and be part of the freedom of the greater first-year experience, the course was not always the students' top priority in terms of time, commitment, or awareness. As a result, in the second year greater emphasis was placed on experiential and interactive exercises, making the course more spontaneous and attractive. One example of such an exercise is the "Building An Idea" project, in which the students, working in their Prides, were asked to assemble the tallest freestanding structure they could conceive and execute in 45 minutes using only spaghetti and miniature marshmallows.

Another class exercise is "Dollars from Lemons," a takeoff on the traditional lemonade stand. In this exercise, each Pride must create and execute a money-making project, using nothing but lemons and derivatives from lemons, supplies ordinarily existing in a student's everyday life, their creativity, and up to twenty dollars borrowed (with interest) from the CIE LC bank (that has to be repaid regardless of result). The goal is to raise as much money as possible from the projects, with half the proceeds donated to charity. The other half is made available to the CIE LC for programming.

The Provocateur Series

This is a series of regularly scheduled evening events bringing faculty members from across the disciplines (e.g., Professor Liz Liddy from the School of Information Studies on technology and business start-ups, particularly from a woman's perspective) together with participants from the "real world" (e.g., Jeff Stamp, formerly the "Idea Guru" of Eureka! Ranch, and Red Dog Martin, a designer and implementer/facilitator of idea generation at Proctor & Gamble) to challenge the students' perceptions and thought processes in the areas of new idea creation and development.

Entrepreneurship at the Movies

Students may attend regularly scheduled movies with themes of creativity, innovation, and entrepreneurship (e.g., *October Sky*, *Metropolis*, and *Gattaca*) preceded and concluded by group discussions led by faculty members with an interest in the subject matter.

Mentoring and Jam Sessions

Originally, these were weekly blocks of open discussion time with the CIE LC director and outside entrepreneurs, during which there was a free flow of thought and discussion about students' entrepreneurial ideas and visions of the world and their lives. The lack of structure, however, turned out to be a demotivating force for first-year students. This approach is now embodied in regular meetings during which each Pride comes as a group to the CIE LC director's home to make dinner and have a more socially centered experience. Open discussion happens more easily, and students are also rewarded with a home-cooked meal.

Social Entrepreneurship

There has been significant engagement of the student Prides as part of a long-term initiative of the Falcone Center outreach arm of the Entrepreneurship and Emerging Enterprises Department in SU's Whitman School, as well as SU as a whole, to implement a model for economic redevelopment for Syracuse's South Side. Known as the South Side Entrepreneurial Connect Project (SSECP), it has introduced CIE LC students to business elements and innovative community service through Pride-based pairings with early-stage emerging businesses and their owner-entrepreneurs. The students become involved through consulting projects, initiation of Internet and other marketing projects, and implementation of discrete tasks to assist local entrepreneurs in reaching their goals.

Ideation Lab

Held five times each semester, this interactive lab introduces methods for exploring and learning new ways to think about, see, and implement idea growth and problem-solving opportunities. Subjects might include nanotechnology, futuring, mind mapping, or convergent and divergent thinking. Each Ideation Lab starts with a participatory lecture and involves application of the principles of that lecture to an in-class, interactive activity.

Social Events

The first semester begins with a white-water rafting retreat on the Black River in the Adirondack Mountains as a team-building exercise. At the end of each semester an open house is held, to which faculty members from across the university are invited. Students give presentations on the semester's work and CIE LC awards are presented. A series of field trips to areas of cultural and artistic interest (such as a trip to a major city cultural center) and interactions with other university academic programs are planned for the future.

Retention and the CIE LC Mentors Program

In order to encourage students to remain in the CIE LC for a second year, it is important to provide ongoing, progressive content designed specifically for them. Sophomores are expected to enroll in a CIE LC independent study, under the tutelage of the CIE LC faculty advisor, that combines their specific fields of study and passion with a meaningful project involving innovation with an entrepreneurial mindset.

Of the active first- and second-year classes in the CIE LC, the retention rate was approximately 33%.[3] Members of the first sophomore class were asked to formulate their independent studies so as to engage subject matter that would coincide with the goals of the SSECP. Some students formed new groups to pursue actual business ventures that they planned to initiate in their junior year and will work through the Falcone Center student business incubator for this purpose. We hope to see more actual business ventures in coming classes.

Program Assessment

There are several major issues that exist generally and unavoidably with each incoming group in its first year.

They are first-year students. This means, particularly in the first semester, that in addition to the CIE LC they are inundated with many new experiences and a host of different opportunities that compete for their time. This is exacerbated by being away from home (many for the first time) and learning how to deal with their freedom while making good decisions.

They come from many schools and colleges within the university. The diversity of the group, seen as a potential strength of the program, also

---

[3] Of the original 78 CIE members, the "active group" was reduced to 46 by the second semester. The reduction was a combined result of students' lack of awareness of their enrollment request (with parents sometimes making a learning community request on a student's behalf) and the ordinary attrition of school transfers, greater focus in other areas, and lack of commitment to the particular CIE program. In the second year, 18 students re-enrolled.

results in different kinds of schedules (e.g., VPA and Newhouse students often have six-hour studios starting either in the morning, early afternoon, or late afternoon, and on different days), workloads, and course requirements. This makes full-group scheduling nearly impossible, except during CIE LC class time (which the different schools and colleges have now incorporated in their class scheduling matrices), on Saturdays (when students generally want to sleep late), or on Sunday evenings (which typically are reserved by the RAs for mandatory floor meetings and Office of Residence Life events).

They may lack in commitment. Most first-year students have not yet established a particular focus or commitment. They do not understand or appreciate the level of commitment expected by the CIE LC when they sign up, sometimes even after full disclosure and discussion. This is clear even on the most basic level, such as their understanding of the importance of checking their SU email account and Blackboard class management system on a daily basis.

What Has Worked

Much of the programming has been very effective and well received by the CIE LC participants. Here are some of the success stories.

- *Interactive exercises.* The "Dollars from Lemons" project, "Building an Idea," and a scavenger hunt all work because they are "in the moment." These kinds of interactive exercises feel less like work and more like play for the students.
- *The best speakers.* Guests like Jeff Stamp and Red Dog Martin, who generate excitement and demand participation through well planned exercises, skits, and music—and are related to products and events relevant to the lives of the students—are the best speakers. Speakers who are not dynamic or who are focused solely on businesses that have no relevance to the students or their current lives are usually tolerated by most and perhaps appreciated by a few, but do not generally promote involvement and engagement. They are perceived as "work": burdensome, and in some cases even irrelevant.
- *Controversial discussion topics.* After a controversy about using lemons in a way symbolic of breasts in an innovative promotion of fundraising for the Breast Cancer Society (with its approval), there was a spirited classroom discussion on whether the method was creative or in bad taste. The discussion was brilliant and passionate, raising many issues of tolerance, awareness, and discrimination. The same was true during a class discussion on ethics in preparation for writing a personal mission statement. Topics that

are controversial or give the students an opportunity to engage with subject matter of importance to them are more likely to engender meaningful and widespread participation.

- *The rafting trip.* This is a fun team-building event that stretches many of the students outside their comfort zone.
- *Mentoring dinners.* These have been a big success as they give the students time out of the residence hall and away from the dining halls. The "home" environment creates a great opportunity for reinforcing the student–instructor relationship, and having the students assist in the preparation of the meal not only promotes team-building but, by its nature, gets them involved in the event.
- *Movie nights.* In the first year, movies were scheduled at 9 p.m., and it was rather hit or miss—more miss. In the second year, the movie time was moved up to 7 p.m. and film selection was based more on student interest. Equally important, participation was increased greatly by the addition of pizza, wings, and soda.
- *Finding student leaders early.* This year, a delegation policy was instituted by creating tech, multimedia, and programming teams headed by a sophomore mentor and at least one strong freshman. This arrangement serves the purposes of recognizing leaders by giving them specific responsibility and creating a pyramidal base of participation.

What Has Not Worked, or Not Worked Consistently

Conversely, several aspects of the program represent opportunities to improve the students' LC experience moving forward.

- *The Ideation Lab.* While about half of the Ideation Labs have been well received, half have not. Two things need to change. First, the emphasis on product development has to be lessened, with greater emphasis placed on innovative thought. Second, the lab needs to rely more on creative, hands-on activities, rather than lectures and slide shows.
- *The South Side Entrepreneurial Connect Project.* The students who are most interested (about 10 to 15) generally prefer to do hands-on social activities involving construction (like playgrounds), from which they get immediate gratification. Some already are involved through school in community work (e.g., working in elementary school programs). Most students do not see the relevance of the SSECP because of its geographical remoteness, and their lack of interest is exacerbated by transportation and scheduling issues.

- *Entrepreneurship course content.* While some interest can be generated in spot discussions or lectures on entrepreneurial methodology or academic content, these topics hold relatively little appeal for students. Most seem to want more specific hands-on or real experience in starting a business.
- *Communication.* Consistent communication is nearly impossible without the support of floor leaders vested with that responsibility. Effective communication occurs more by word of mouth and announcements posted at the elevators than by any other means. For the first-year students, too much advance notice is frequently ineffective.
- *Presence on the floor.* Generally, the faculty advisor would be on the floor twice a week for class and at least one other event. In the fall, this level of presence was augmented by the mentoring dinner, which was an excellent way to connect with the students. Unplanned visits were unsuccessful, as the students were not receptive to impromptu meetings that involved just sitting around and talking, and scheduling meetings for specific purposes on the floor were always complicated by the diversity of schedules.

Suggested Improvements

In an ideal situation, in addition to a faculty member who has the time and desire to spend several hours a week with the CIE LC, a graduate student would live on the floor. If this were not possible, then the full-time commitment of a graduate student who could make the CIE part of, or the focus of, efforts in research and other academic pursuits would be the next best arrangement.

The CIE LC program has a number of minimally invested faculty and other consultants performing discrete tasks. This creates a risk of discontinuity and an implicit lack of authority, despite the fact that the diversity of faculty is a huge plus from the perspective of the students. Stability would also be enhanced through improved screening of the students serving as upper-class mentors.

Research into best practices reveals that all of the existing national entrepreneurship learning communities that show success have a dedicated team of people whose full-time work is the LC. Typically, that involves having at least one full-time faculty leader (some of whom live in the residence hall, as they do at Oregon State University) with at least one full-time administrative assistant. None of the programs studied involve first-year students. All involve applications and rewards for academic achievement and demonstrated commitment to entrepreneurship, typically arising out of the particular university's business, engineering, or technology schools. They also involve upper-class students and graduate students who have earned the right to partici-pate because of their academic achievement.

While those who are involved in Syracuse University's Barbara Glazer Weinstein and Jerome S. Glazer Creativity, Innovation, and Entrepreneurship Learning Community continue to believe in the innovative potential of the SU model in seeking to retain the involvement of non-residential student members after their sophomore year, we will not be able to evaluate the extent of its success until we go through a full four-year cycle. More time is necessary to better understand retention through the four years, and to see the impact of developed relationships with upper-class mentors as they evolve in entre-preneurship and as moral leaders of the community. We also believe it will be important to develop internships and other opportunities to encourage new business start-up exposure for the upper-class students.

Diversity and Citizenship

Silvio Torres-Saillant and James Duah-Agyeman

OVER the past decade, higher education in the United States has significantly addressed the need to promote ongoing development of knowledge, awareness, and anti-oppression skills to function within the ever-diversifying campuses across the nation. Learned observers have established that despite perceptions of ethnic equality, we live in a society that continues to place individuals in positions of advantage or disadvantage in relation to their race and ethnicity. At the same time, students across the country, irrespective of origin, seem to share a common reticence regarding cross-cultural discussions. As a result, institutions of higher learning nationwide must confront the challenge of creating appropriate environments wherein students may find it safe and rewarding to engage in the difficult conversations that the matter entails.

We feel we have made meaningful headway toward the creation of such an environment at Syracuse University, particularly for first-year students enrolling in the Multicultural Living-Learning Community (MLLC). Through a collaboration between the Office of Residence Life, the College of Arts and Sciences, and the Office of Multicultural Affairs, we have offered a three-credit course, "Living in a Diverse Society" (LAS 300), every fall since 2002, with considerable success. The course posits that living in a diverse society in the early twenty-first century requires the ability to interact with difference and the willingness to entertain ideas that challenge our most basic assumptions about humanity and our fellow citizens. The democratic ideal that the modern world upholds can come to fruition only through the recognition of and respect for diversity as a fundamental value. Acceptance of diversity is not a courtesy that we extend to others. Rather, it is something that we do for ourselves; through such an acceptance we enter into a fuller, more harmonious, and less distorted relationship with the objective reality of our world. The modern citizen understands diversity as a sign of a well-balanced and healthy atmosphere.

Consider the metaphor of humanity as a garden, as found in the words of

'Abdu'l-Bahá, promoter of the teachings of the Bahai community, an interfaith religious organization. We all welcome the spectacle of a garden in which the celebration of difference dominates. We delight in the charm and beauty resulting from "the joyous contrast of colour" that comes from the bringing together of "flowers of every hue, form and perfume." Besides displaying its own beauty, "each flower, each tree, each fruit" brings out the qualities of the others. However, we do not appreciate the same phenomenon as easily when we encounter it in the human family; hence, the author bids us to regard "those of different race and colour" from ourselves as we would "different coloured roses growing in the beautiful garden of humanity and rejoice to be among them." Insofar as the roads that lead to truth are many, this includes "those whose opinions differ from [our] own" ('Abdu'l-Bahá, 1912/1972, pp. 52–53). Unfortunately, most of us inherit cultural histories, social systems, and communal traditions that understand sameness as a prerequisite to group membership and, consequently, have tended to regard differences as threats to unity.

Educators therefore cannot assume that students coming to our campuses will have mastered the skills or embraced the outlook that our diverse society demands of its citizens. Since overcoming homogenizing instincts should be one of the indispensable benefits of higher education, we strongly believe in exposing students to the study of diversity as an academic subject in order to equip them with the analytical tools necessary for identifying the ideologies, schemes of thought, and conceptual paradigms sustaining the exclusionary behaviors that emanate from homogenizing thought. Our course introduces students to the serious consideration of different cultural forms, lifestyles, political ideologies, religious beliefs, philosophies, artistic traditions, sexual orientations, worldviews, and other aspects of human expression that they will find in modern society. Students examine the ongoing tension between the concrete diversity they witness in their world and the persistence of homogeneity as a principle that continues to have currency among those with the power and influence to impose particular definitions of national identity. An Anglophone monolingual desire continues to exert influence over the American national imaginary despite the multiplicity of languages historically and currently on the tongues of the American population. Considering, for instance, that Spanish was spoken and written in what is now the United States for nearly one hundred years prior to the arrival of the first English-speaking settlers to Jamestown, Virginia, in 1607, the recent furor caused by the immigrant rally organizers who dared to produce a Spanish rendition of the "Star-Spangled Banner" would seem a bit misplaced.

"Living in a Diverse Society" consists of lectures, readings, site visits, guest presentations by specialists, class discussions, and other activities all aimed at eliciting thought, conversation, and writing about numerous aspects of the overall subject of diversity. The course insists on diversifying the notion of diversity so that the focus on race and ethnicity remains important, but does not monopolize the attention of the class. With that goal in mind, we look at definitions of the family in light of our awareness of sexual and personal realities that challenge nuclear and heteronormative assumptions. The recent debates over gay marriage, which brought into collision opposing views concerning who may legally constitute a family unit, will come in handy the next time the course is offered. The course typically examines various understandings of the here and hereafter in light of dissimilar conceptions of the divine. The teachings of Karen Armstrong about the essence of the religious life have been useful in past semesters to organize discussions about some shared principles upheld by most faiths. In the fall of 2005, anthropologist Susan S. Wadley, a South Asia specialist, offered an introduction to the religious cosmology of India that awakened many students from their complacent "familiarity" with the form and nature of the divine. Similarly, the course compares the varied scales of value implicit in different socioeconomic systems (capitalism, socialism, etc.) while examining culturally specific worldviews and philosophies of history with their distinct emphases on destiny, the purpose of existence, the value of a human life, progress, civilization, and the place of the individual. The ideas of love and goodness coming from different religious cosmologies also enter the discussion.

The course studies representations of the beautiful with a focus on cross-cultural and epochal appreciations of attractiveness in the human body as well as the lure of homogenizing ideals that cause people to undergo cosmetic surgery in pursuit of fitting the prevailing standards. The fact that women are more emphatically subject to such pressures than men also provokes reflection about the concrete effect of symbolic politics on the less empowered. A gender module figures among the most successful features of the course. Students quickly learn to see homogenizing practices at work—not only, for instance, in salary discrepancies between male and female workers with similar skills, but also in the standard architectural design of malls and movie theaters, such that women are frequently obliged to stand in line to use bathroom facilities while men can speedily restore their comfort level without a wait. Overall, the course concentrates on the inevitable coexistence of dissimilar, distinct, and contrasting systems of value in the cultures, constituencies, linguistic groups, class origins, identities, and differentiated communities represented in the population of the United States and other contemporary societies.

Because a course as intellectually and socially ambitious as ours cannot afford to rely solely on the learning, experience, and approach of a single instructor, we have drawn on wide-ranging areas of expertise, bodies of knowledge, schools of thought, ideological perspectives, teaching styles, and ways of learning. We thus represent diversity in the form as well as the content of what we study, acknowledging difference even in the transmission of information. The areas of expertise represented include history, disability studies, women's studies, anthropology, religion, sociology, literature, film, ethnic studies, art, and LGBT (Lesbian, Gay, Bisexual, and Transgender) studies. Experts from the various fields of knowledge are integrated into the course through guest lectures and presentations. To make the fully inter-disciplinary structure of the course automatic and integral rather than dependent upon the instructor's ability to enlist the contributions of colleagues, we have contemplated an arrangement whereby the course may be taught not by an instructor, but by a conglomerate of pertinent academic units, each contributing the modules corresponding to their fields. We are, at present, in the planning stages of that projected new arrangement, and we hope its final implementation will provide a model that other interdisciplinary initiatives would wish to emulate.

Though our efforts have met with success, we feel surest of our accomplishments whenever we believe we have witnessed a discernible transformation in the thinking of our students, when we have the impression that diversity matters to them beyond the fulfillment of the course requirements, and when we see that it matters to them as modern citizens mindful of their society's promise to advance the cause of democratic inclusion for the benefit of all segments of the population. We realize, of course, that a course can do only so much. But we are counting on more than just our course. As the university continues to enhance its commitment to diversity by translating its inclusive philosophy into sustained action, students will gather from the pervasive ethos of our institution the very ideas and practices they need to live efficiently and humanely in a diverse society. As that trend continues, courses such as ours will primarily serve the function of organizing pertinent knowledge for our students and giving them a language with which to communicate the precepts our campus teaches them inside and outside of the classroom.

References

'Abdu'l-Bahá. (1972). *Paris talks.* London: Baha'i Publishing Trust. (Original work published 1912)

Creating Change and Continuity in Your Learning Community

Paul Buckley

WHEN I began working for the Multicultural Living-Learning Community (MLLC) of Syracuse University as a graduate student, I walked into an organization rich in potential but hindered by confusion amongst its leaders. The MLLC, a partnership between the Office of Multicultural Affairs (OMA), the Office of Residence Life (ORL), and faculty, was only three years old. I was excited and anxious about the contributions I could make as a representative of the Office of Multicultural Affairs. However, I quickly realized that the organization could not move forward until it recognized and overcame the obstacles to its success. The evolution of the program in the years since is a testament to persistence in developing collaborative relationships, exploring innovative ideas, making courageous decisions, and negotiating leadership within a partnership.

Background

Syracuse University created its Multicultural Living-Learning Community in the fall of 2000 to provide students with an atmosphere that would encourage them to nurture inquisitiveness and enlightenment, with the ultimate goal of assisting them "to respect, appreciate, and celebrate multiculturalism and diversity in all its forms" (Duah-Agyeman, 2004, p. 121). The organizers of this learning community included students, faculty, and administrators, making it a unique partnership from the beginning. The concept also had the support of OMA and ORL. Amnat Chittaphong, a charter member of the MLLC, became the project's graduate instructor and coordinator. Chittaphong worked within an administrative structure that included two coordinating offices (OMA and ORL), an advisory board, faculty and staff mentors, student mentors, and a resident advisor.

This leadership plan sufficed when the program was in its infancy, but the introduction of new elements in the summer of 2002 challenged the dynamic. It was then that I began my work with the MLLC in collaboration with another graduate assistant from OMA. At about the same time, a new resident director and a new resident advisor were assigned to the MLLC floor, located in Haven Hall on the SU campus. Additionally, a new three-credit course in the College of Arts and Sciences (LAS 300: Living in a Diverse Society) was developed and initiated in the fall. Previously, the MLLC course for first-year students had been considered a seminar class. Things were changing. People were changing. It was inevitable that the MLLC would have to change, too.

Shared Responsibility, Shared Ambiguity

Partnerships are often simultaneously challenging and rewarding. They are dynamic and reflect the character and tone of the relationships among all involved. Partnerships can be particularly challenging when they exist within a matrix of independent and overlapping entities and bureaucracies, such as those involved in the MLLC during the 2002–2003 academic year. The most frequently asked question during that pivotal year seemed to be, "Whose responsibility is this?"

It was unclear in the fall of 2002 whether the original leadership structure existed. Further ambiguity surrounded the decision-making power of the project's current staff. Work was complicated by shifting views of leadership and the "coordinator." Who was it? Was it the OMA director? One of the OMA graduate assistants? Was it the residence director? Which one of the graduate assistants should the Office of Learning Communities director call first? Should the full-time professional staff maintain greater responsibility and supervision for the project? Should a part-time staff member, a graduate assistant, coordinate this project and give direction to full-time staff members? These questions were not always articulated, yet they remained implicit and informed every meeting, particularly when decisions had to be made.

I was empowered by my supervisor to coordinate the program on behalf of my office. However, as a graduate assistant I had to operate within the university system, which traditionally reserves power for full-time professionals and often privileges academic colleagues, especially those with tenure. The politics of our collaboration was further complicated by the need to make decisions about resources. Each time, we had to learn through trial and error which person was indeed responsible for individual tasks. With the metaphorical ball clearly on the court, we were always negotiating whose turn it was to dribble and pass, or who had the right to shoot. Basketball can be fun or frustrating depending on how you play and who you are playing with. The same can be said of learning communities.

Students also desired clarity about the MLLC. What was this learning community? What did program administrators expect from those who participated? What were the academic expectations for the MLLC and how would overall performance be measured? What should students expect of themselves? While the MLLC charter expressed particular goals and objectives, clear and consistent communication to the students about the experience of that first year did not exist. This compounded issues of accountability for student participation in outside-classroom learning and community-building activities.

Moving Forward Together

In the second year of my work with the MLLC, I began conducting a qualitative research project, interviewing several students about their experiences with the learning community. Though this research was part of my degree program, the data I collected became significant for me professionally and gave me a better sense of students' perceptions of their experiences and of the ways that learning could be improved. It also gave me the confidence and the credibility to assert my position as the coordinator and to guide decisions that would reshape the MLLC.

In this second year, being the sole coordinator for the MLLC at Haven Hall allowed me to organize MLLC activities in a different way and to collaborate creatively with my colleague in OMA. For instance, I learned from the research that cliques existed in the community. First-year MLLC students were concerned that "returners" (students who returned to the MLLC for a second year) tended to keep to themselves and were less active in some of the community-wide projects and assignments. I observed some of that separation and apathy in my research and in my daily interactions with the community. Further, I was concerned that some of the returning students might be using the MLLC solely as a social opportunity, rather than an intellectual experience that could broaden their multicultural competence.

Recognizing that some of the challenges I faced on the administrative level were fueled by attachments to the older ways of doing things, I sought to maximize the development of new ideas in the community and allow new students to have the best chance for a positive experience. I also had to recognize the need to shift the context of my authority in the community so that, as coordinator, I could have more impact (on this issue, see Moore, 1993). Hence, I consider my decision to limit the number of returning students one of the most crucial changes to the program. I capped the number at ten students, 25% of the total MLLC population. Additionally, I interviewed each candidate about the MLLC's evolution and need for change, and the important role that returning students play in modeling positive behavior to new students. These tactics proved useful in creating a learning community comprised of students who would be willing to embrace new expectations. The Office of Learning

Communities director was particularly helpful in this process, supporting my decisions and remaining open to the results.

The following year yielded several rewards, despite ongoing challenges. Enrollment in the LAS 300 course was up, participation in MLLC activities increased, and the returning students promoted a stronger sense of community and "intergenerational" communication. I attribute these improvements to clearer communication of expectations to all parties. Efforts at better communication included a modified description of the MLLC in marketing materials to incoming students; open communication about roles and assignments for MLLC staff; development of the "MLLC Pledge," which states a clearer list of expectations; discussion and integration of MLLC goals; and more consistent "frontline team" meetings involving the coordinator, residence director, and resident assistant.

Three years after beginning my work with the MLLC, I took the post of associate director for the Office of Multicultural Affairs. In my role as a full-time professional in the office, I provided direction to the graduate assistant who coordinated the MLLC project and negotiated its partnerships. This arrangement and change in my position allowed me further to develop ideas for the project, focusing on the structure rather than the coordination of activities. It also gave me the authority to see that ideas are implemented. For example, I limited even further the number of MLLC returning students to six. I then developed a structured experience called the MLLC Ambassadors Program, which allows returning students to serve as co-chairs on three committees that assist in facilitating greater participation among all MLLC students. These committee assignments include community service, public relations, and programming.

As a result of these changes, the MLLC is a healthy community of learners who are innovators, explorers, and active citizens beyond the eleventh floor of Haven Hall. They fully engage the opportunities they have been given in this experience and, in so doing, challenge the MLLC staff to consider new ideas and explore reasons for the old. I have learned that innovation ages quickly. Community building must always respond to the current concerns and issues of community members. Hence, learning communities, especially those that engage multiculturalism, are in constant flux. New minds demand new pedagogical practices, different languages to frame current concerns, and, always, openness to their own investments. The partnership with ORL and faculty has grown stronger as all sides communicate more openly about the development of the MLLC project and ideas for greater achievements. With varying actors in the partnership (due to staff changes), it has been important to articulate clearly the roles that must be filled for successful collaboration and a successful learning community.

References

Duah-Agyeman, J. K. (2004). Multicultural living/learning community: By the students, for the students. In S. N. Hurd & R. F. Stein (Eds.), *Building and sustaining learning communities* (pp. 120–129). Bolton, MA: Anker.

Moore, P. L. (1993). The political dimension of decision making. In M. J. Barr (Ed.), *The handbook of student affairs administration* (pp. 422–434). Needham Heights, MA: Jossey-Bass.

Learning Community
Encounters and Strategies for
Effective Teaching Assistantship

Jamie Kathleen Portillo

As a Ph.D. candidate and former teaching assistant (TA) for the Department of Anthropology at Syracuse University's Maxwell School, I have embarked on an academic career that revolves around understanding the world from a variety of perspectives. In my three years as a TA, I derived great pleasure teaching and learning from Syracuse undergraduates—whom I consider an inquisitive and enthusiastic group of fashion-forward, pop-culture-savvy and politically correct citizens. Admittedly, prior to teaching an Anthropology of Global Encounters course to a freshmen-level learning community, I had settled into a comfortable rhythm both in my teaching style and in the level of scholarship I expected from my students. When I was asked to lead a discussion section composed entirely of Social Justice Learning Community members, I was honored; however, even with the gracious introduction provided by the Office of Learning Communities itself, I found myself strategically unprepared for the challenge that lay ahead.

The Social Justice Learning Community was composed of roughly 20 freshman honors students who lived on the same dorm floor and who took at least two classes together. The nature of the learning community (LC) was to prepare students for careers in law and medicine—fields typically requiring ethics training. Aside from the anthropology class, students also participated in another class, Ethics and Value Theory, which required a volume of reading from Plato to Hobbes, Kant to Nietzsche, with a smattering of Herskovitz, Linton, and Rawls. The Global Encounters course included an intense introduction to professional and ethical dilemmas in anthropology through Rob Borofsky's online, interactive book *Yanomami: The Fierce Controversy and What We Can Learn from It*. (The "fierce controversy" of the subtitle is that surrounding geneticist James Neel and anthropologist Napoleon Chagnon's studies among and subsequent representation of Brazilian and Venezuelan Yanomami people, often cited as classic examples of unethical ethnographic research.) I was excited by the idea of supplementing my 50-minute, twice-weekly discussion sections with their ancient-to-modern philosophy reader and other LC experiences. These augmented lessons, I assumed, would also be useful for my "regular" teaching section, consisting of unacquainted students at various educational levels enrolled solely in the Global Encounters course.

I was wrong. Furthermore, working as a teaching assistant for this group proved far more demanding than expected. Collectively, the community demonstrated ambitious learning strategies and varying interpretations of social justice depending on their personal and academic inclinations. Most students operated at what I would consider an accelerated learning level relative to their non-LC peers. Thus, I felt it necessary to prepare two separate lesson plans per week, fearing that my regular section discussions would have been trite and uninspiring to the LC section, to say the least. The LC students also vigorously engaged with and invested significant time in their assign-ments, thronging to my office hours and making additional appointments to read over numerous topic paper drafts and to discuss projects—and even to expound upon personal issues surrounding and informing their class work. As a graduate student at a research-based institution, I was prepared to handle this level of interaction in ethnographic research; I was unprepared, however, for the extra time commitment and mental stamina required of me by my teaching section. I regularly complained of feeling proverbially overworked and underpaid.

That semester challenged me practically, pedagogically, and personally. Executing lesson plans and evaluating academic progress (i.e., grading) for both LC and regular discussion section students presented additional time-management concerns. While typically alleviating discussion inhibitions, the intimate nature of the LC necessitated structural and ethical considerations for debating contentious issues in class. Finally, maintaining a "professional" student–teacher relationship risked alienating students who anticipated a similar, personal interaction with their TA as with their Resident Associate and their peers. As the semester progressed, the intimate nature of the classroom experience did allow opportunity to interact with students on a personal level. Sitting in a circle on most days facilitated eye contact, and I could discern who was familiar with whom. I observed the formation of friendships and alliances between some students, and also the exclusion of others from particular groups. But, generally, the closeness of the learning community seemed to prevail over discussion inhibitions.

This dynamic had its pros and cons. Some students interpreted our free-flowing style of conversation as license to interrupt and talk over others with whom they disagreed. I encountered some difficulty managing casual conversation eruptions, and although the discussions were mostly centered on relevant topics, they nevertheless distracted the class as a whole. Initially, I hesitated to suspend such spontaneity unless another student was trying to address the class, because I appreciated students' enthusiasm and felt they were taking responsibility for their own learning. Yet, despite having included in my section syllabus the guidelines for participating in classroom discussions, by the middle of the semester it became necessary to reiterate common classroom etiquette. In retrospect, I most certainly should have provided a more disciplined classroom structure for these freshman students, especially as I began to observe these same students' inattention during lecture.

In addition to emerging friendships and alliances, I also witnessed the materialization of individual "personalities" throughout the semester. One such personality in particular proved troublesome. This student regularly espoused what I perceived as bigoted and borderline-racist opinions that distressed some students from ethnic minority backgrounds. Furthermore, throughout this writing-intensive course, this student regularly transformed his papers into political platforms—which I subsequently marked down for not following the assignment. As a result, his strategy for improving his class performance evolved from ranting into "telling me what I wanted to hear," placing caveats before paragraphs and disclaimers in the footnotes stating his *actual* position. I challenged him to delve into stereotypes, to explain what they meant rather than using loaded descriptions, and to think beyond limited frameworks and loaded language. I also elicited other students' responses to his ideas. When those methods had no effect, I implored the student at least to consider the conceptual and actual dangers posed by such "borderline" thinking.

This was a mistake. Because he displayed such charisma, other students began to rally around this individual, exalting him like a notorious celebrity or even a "class clown." In my mid-semester evaluations, three comments under areas I could improve upon suggested I provide a space where "both sides" of an argument can be heard. For the first time in my academic career, I was being accused of censorship, bias, and favoritism (for those students who understood the material and demonstrated their comprehension, per the traditional student–teacher dynamic). The majority of students, however, asserted that they enjoyed the liberties of free dialogue that could be had in the section. Thus, my dilemmas were twofold: how to curtail this individual's commentary without diminishing the quality, and indeed purpose, of classroom discussions, and how to continue to provide a space where all perspectives could be shared and learned from.

My solution was to resist engaging with this student's strong political and personal opinions as I had been doing, and instead to characterize this student's view as only one way of thinking among others, just like the theoretical, philosophical, and political expressions of the ethnographers whose work we read in class. I encouraged other students to respond to him, alleviating the pressure of engagement and negative reinforcement, and making him equally accountable to his peers. But I was still shaken. So, rather than offering only my own (and the professor's own) understandings of the books' theoretical components and the lecture material, I felt compelled to prepare "extra material" to ensure that both sides of an argument were presented without a bias against what I considered to be the dominant ideologies informing most of our readings. In other words, these primary ethnographic texts, whose ultimate purpose in the course was to substantiate critiques of unethical practice in research including human subjects, were now presented in such a way that students had to evaluate them for themselves *sans* the anthropologist's perspective.

Beyond even ethics, there were troubles. Due to the nature of our readings, some of which exposed students to, for example, cultural practices among Haitians that complicated the prevention of HIV/AIDS in their society, it became exceedingly difficult to be "objective" and still effectively present the course material. After repeatedly clashing with several other opinionated students, I became aware that when engaging in critical discourse, there are no objective, politically neutral ways of presenting information. The reality that (even after Herskovitz) these budding scholars were not comfortable accepting an anthropological, culturally relative approach to understanding other cultures was difficult to accept. By the end of the semester, I realized that my responsibility for communicating the material was to promote an understanding of, not necessarily an agreement with, those concepts. I had never encountered this difficulty with any other group of students, and I attributed the experience to the character of this particular learning community.

I am hopeful that my semester-long travails will prove insightful to future teaching assistants considering involvement in a learning community, as well as to those who wish to construct a mutually beneficial learning experience. Teaching a learning community section was an ultimately gratifying, albeit stressful, experience for me, as it challenged my normal boundaries in the student–teacher relationship and made me "ready for anything" to come. I sometimes felt as if the learning community students expected a more personal interaction with me due to our relative closeness in age and my status as a teaching assistant rather than a professor. However, due to my perceived need to maintain composure and control, I never felt entirely comfortable relinquishing a professional classroom role. Consequently, I feel I may have alienated some of my students as persons rather than as students by coming across as stuffy or even calloused. With this perspective, I hope to reorient my attitude towards future students and to make clear that, although my purpose was to instruct, I did indeed relish the opportunity for one-on-one interactions.

I have also learned some valuable lessons about teaching ethics to a small, hand-selected group of students whose academic career trajectories were in medicine and law, not the core liberal arts group to whom I was accustomed.

The first lesson is pedagogical, and involves thinking carefully through my own positionality (a postmodern term ethnographers use to inform readers about their own understandings, biases, and agendas) before presenting contentious issues in class. Our students had not traveled the winding road to the reflexive turn in anthropology, but they were still expected to navigate through ethnography's corollary of multiple, subaltern voices. In retrospect, I realize now that the age-old demon of objectivist versus interpretivist science had reared its ugly head, and I hadn't the hermeneutic weaponry to slay the beast. These students' Truths had to be solid, defensible, made *real*. They had to not only understand the objectives of the original researchers (i.e., Chagnon and Neel), the accusations against the pair, and the consequences for the Yanomami themselves, but they had to be able to come to *their own* conclusions that the research was somehow unethical. Most took nothing at face value.

The second lesson was to anticipate the needs of a teaching position before saying, "Yes, I'll do it!" In retrospect, agreeing to teach this particular recitation without prior knowledge, training, or experience with learning communities was my first indiscretion. I was asked by the professor teaching the 200+ Global Encounters class if I would like to teach the learning community section based on my previous TA experience for Global Encounters. With a different instructor, however, the course material and schedule was unfamiliar to me—indeed, I had a learning curve. I strongly recommend that teaching assistants know what they are getting into before following in my footsteps. My failure to conduct a more thorough "background check" at the beginning of the semester may have prevented me from better negotiating the classroom setting later in the year. I would highly recommend taking the time to create a student information sheet, one that includes basic get-to-know-yous like favorite books and films, but also information pertaining to the epistemological inclinations and proclivities of your students. For example, in this particular class I could have asked: what are ethics? Are there any universal ethics? What ethical considerations should be given to human (and, perhaps, non-human) research subjects? Right off the bat, this would have given me important clues to how my class understood the issues at hand.

My second suggestion is that TAs should try to understand their audiences and to meet them halfway. Each of our students follows a unique path based on past experiences, present influences, and future goals. As instructors, we often seek to create those experiences (at least in the classroom) and to influence our students according to our own discipline-specific and personal positions, all toward the goal of higher education. But what I am advocating is a more back-of-the-classroom exchange between us and our students, so we might mutually situate our respective intellectual appointments rather than establishing them hammer and nail. By showing genuine consideration for even the most "stubborn" views, we can negotiate for intellectual trust and gain the respect deserving of someone in a position of authority. And yes, I do believe that even as TAs we should work on building a positive and assertive classroom presence.

My third and final suggestion concerns my isolation. Lacking a support group or sounding board to evaluate classroom "episodes" (the euphemism I now fondly use to refer to them) forced me to rely solely on my individual intuition. This could have been avoided had I made better use of my department. Teaching assistants should utilize mentoring relationships and peer networks to discuss their difficulties. Further, TAs should have at their disposal an LC liaison to guide their instruction as well as to put them in touch with other previous or current LC TAs. As an aside, many TAs, in addition to working on their advanced degrees, find themselves teaching two sections per semester. Given the potential additional workload that teaching an LC section presents, would it be logistically out of the question for departments to "count" that one section as a two-course load?

These are learning moments to be shared amongst colleagues and professors. I hope that my experience encourages the future formation of a support network for teaching assistants in learning community sections, and ultimately engenders a new *modus operandi* for TAs in learning community settings.

Bridging the Gap
Constructing Faculty–Student
Relationships for Mutual Learning

Braden Smith and Rachel Smith

THE ideal achievement of undergraduate instruction is engaged classrooms—learning environments in which knowledge is generated not only through the transmission of knowledge from teacher to student, but from student to student, and from student to teacher (Barr & Tagg, 1995). In such an environment learners not only receive knowledge but become capable of generating their own knowledge, assessing it critically, and sharing it with their peers. It is an environment where every student feels comfortable contributing, where every student can ask questions, and where self-directed study emerges as a natural by-product of the instructional experience—part of what Noel Entwistle (2000) calls "deep learning." Not only do students take from these experiences a deeper knowledge of the subjects, they also generate connections between fellow students and faculty that can serve as transformational social networks. In our experience, colleges that are able to produce these types of experiences for even limited numbers of undergraduates often find that the overall experience of the entire college population benefits. Students become more capable of the type of social agency that can change the nature of the college as an institution and the student body as a society.

That's the good news. The bad news is that the engaged classroom is rarely, if ever, produced naturally. All involved—professors, teaching assistants (TAs), academic and residential college administrators, and especially students—must consciously conceive of, plan, and implement these types of learning experiences. And when developing residential learning community models, they must do so both in and beyond the classroom. Learning communities have emerged as a potentially unique way of engaging students in the learning process by bridging the divide between the students' academic identity and their identity outside the classroom. Planned learning experiences

70

that take place in residential college settings subvert the traditional social roles of professors, TAs, and students, allowing students to engage on a more personal and more meaningful level with the subject under discussion. Challenges to successful learning communities grow, however, from the large gap that exists between faculty and students. Professors are often far removed from students by the traditional barriers that make them authority figures.

The key to bridging this gap, we propose, is the teaching assistant.

TAs already occupy a transitional social role in the academic setting in their dual roles as teachers and students. A well-planned program that systematically uses TAs to link in-classroom instruction with activities and events planned in learning communities can become a powerful way to produce that ever-elusive engaged classroom. As the bridge between students and teachers, TAs can play an important role in sustaining and strengthening the partnerships between faculty, students, and administrators.

An early model of a learning community was the University of Wisconsin at Madison's Experimental College, founded by Alexander Meiklejohn in 1927. Meiklejohn espoused the twin goals of unifying the curriculum by making learning across contexts seamless and lessening the distance between faculty members and students (Nelson, 2001). Although this particular "experiment" was not long-lasting, a seed was planted. More than 70 years later, we (the authors) entered one of UW–Madison's residential learning communities. As undergraduate students, our experiences there shaped our learning and our practice. Both of us were also House Fellows there (similar to the position of resident assistant or RA) before coming to Syracuse University as graduate students. While at Syracuse University, Rachel studied learning communities as part of her master's and doctoral coursework in the Higher Education Program. Braden served as a TA for a course involved in a learning community while studying as a doctoral student in the Political Science Department. From our experiences, we learned that building successful partnerships between in-classroom instruction and residential learning communities involves commitment, creativity, and flexibility on the part of TAs, students, faculty, and administrators. TAs in particular can serve as connecting links between these partners.

Learning communities that successfully integrate social life with academic instruction are rarely produced without a strong commitment to working as a team (Engstrom & Tinto, 2000). Planning and promoting programs designed by residential college administrators or faculty might work, but one-sided planning does not capture the type of engagement that the learning community is supposed to promote. Students should be actively involved in the creation of new programs and events, and TAs should engage their students in dialogue about how to create the best out-of-classroom learning experiences. In planning activities that are designed to bring faculty and TAs together with students in an effort to extend and enhance classroom learning, it might be tempting to fall back upon purely social activities, such as floor pizza parties or basketball games. Activities such as these certainly create less formal student–teacher relationships, but it is difficult to see how they promote the type of "deep learning" that Entwistle describes. Even faculty–staff dinners, where students eat in the cafeteria at a table with a few professors, may not facilitate the creation of better teacher–student relationships, especially if either the students or the teachers are not comfortable with their new roles as peers.

Both the authors, for example, have endured awkward dinners with faculty members who default to lecturing on their particular fields of interest. Meanwhile, students get nervous while eating with "the classroom authority" and revert to the role of passive knowledge recipients. The experience is especially difficult for faculty members who might not have a clear understanding of why they have been asked to participate. Faculty members at UW–Madison who are involved in learning communities are often asked to lead discussions with newly arrived freshmen about how to make meaning out of their college experiences. Although the program is a wonderful idea, our fellow RAs would often exchange horror stories about professors who were too intimidated to say anything, or who were so intent on lecturing that they forgot that students were even there. From our experience, TAs are more capable of adapting to these types of situations because they still have one foot in the world of the average student. That is part of the reason why the participation of TAs in a learning community is so important. TAs can build the bridge between the social world of the student and the academic world of the professor.

Some of the most successful bridge-building activities we experienced involved faculty members or TAs with particular course-related interests they wanted to share with students outside the classroom. This passion helped facilitate deep learning in unusual settings that promoted more honest and comfortable dialogue. One of our professors led an annual sociological bike tour around the city of Madison. Students and faculty met to explore various neighborhoods, their histories, and their current sociological contexts of race and class. Other educational trips included visiting buildings by architect Frank Lloyd Wright to explore architectural design, an inside look at a prison to explore issues of justice, and an outdoor Shakespeare play to study the dramatic arts and literature. Each event was built on the participation of a professor or TA who could provide an educational context. Although these types of activities were rarely connected to specific classes, one can easily imagine similar trips that directly connect particular events to classroom discussions.

As exciting as literally going on journeys together can be, there are other ways to bridge gaps and forge connected classrooms (particularly important since budgetary factors often play a role in the types of opportunities that are available). We remember fondly the connections we made with graduate students through the residential college when we were undergraduates. A few TAs were assigned to each floor of our building, and they came to many social and educational events. They were both similar to and different from us, but we asked them questions and got to know them as people. What was it like to be in graduate school? What sorts of things were they studying? Why? What kind of life did they envision? Being relatively new to the institution, they also had a lot of questions for us about our experiences as students. Although both of us were attracted to graduate study on our own, having the chance to get to know these students made us a little better prepared for our own graduate school experiences and for life as future faculty members.

Since then we have come to appreciate much more the effort these graduate students put into getting to know us and facilitating our learning. And, certainly, it must have taken a great deal of effort considering all of their other obligations, such as teaching, studies, and research. Their participation in the learning community was above and beyond their "normal" jobs. This brings us to our last point. It is important for TAs who might become involved in learning communities to first get to know themselves, what they are comfortable with, and what their own goals are. Participating in a learning community can enrich teaching and learning experiences—imagine the substantive discussions that can be generated in classrooms—but accomplishing these goals takes time. Also, not everyone feels comfortable sharing a purely social space with students; some TAs might find they need a little more distance. Self-exploration can also help TAs discover their strengths in planning for the learning community experience. Learning communities do not fully subvert the roles of teachers and students; there is always some sort of power dynamic. Boundaries exist that probably should not be crossed. However, being involved in a learning community often gives everyone more flexibility to explore knowledge wherever the communal experience takes them.

Again, creating successful partnerships between TAs and learning communities takes work, and unfortunately many TAs are often overwhelmed by the responsibilities of being graduate students. Fortunately, there are ways of making TAs more comfortable with adding even more to their already busy schedules. We have already mentioned a few, but they deserve to be repeated.

First, administrators and student staff (such as those underappreciated RAs) should clearly communicate the type of roles that TAs who are interested in participating might be expected to play. The most stressful part of participating in a learning community is often the uncertainty of the social situations, but this stress can be reduced if administrators clearly articulate the type of relationship and commitment that is expected.

Second, faculty members must also be brought in as partners in the learning community, even if their actual participation might be limited. Obviously, direct and consistent faculty participation is ideal, but even something as simple as generating awareness among the faculty might make a big difference for TAs who want to participate, but who are afraid of making another commitment. We often encountered TAs at UW–Madison who feared that their faculty advisors would frown upon participation in learning communities because it would take time away from research. In our experience, these professors often adopted this view because they saw learning communities as just another social function. Making professors and other college administrators aware of what learning communities are all about—fostering real student learning—is an important way of reducing the costs that many TAs might fear they will incur if they decide to participate.

Finally, not every learning community may be right for every TA. Interested TAs should find out as much as possible about a particular learning community program before volunteering. There are many benefits to participating, and TAs who take some ownership can create experiences that will help them develop their abilities to teach, learn, and relate to students.

The picture we have painted is a complex one, requiring attention to both the planning and the execution of learning in communities. Working with learning communities is challenging and rewarding, and we hope TAs will be excited by the possibilities for engaging with students in what can be truly meaningful ways. Learning communities have impacted the authors both as undergraduates and as graduate students, and they will, in all likelihood, continue to positively influence our teaching and research. We plan to make use of these experiences ourselves as we develop good teaching practices, get to know our students, and develop learning spaces for everyone. Participating in learning communities as teaching assistants can be a learning experience for all involved, and TAs can take from the experience the knowledge of their own crucial role in the communities' success.

References

Barr, R. B., & Tagg, J. (1995). From teaching to learning: A new paradigm for undergraduate education. *Change, 27*(6), 12–25.

Engstrom, C. M., & Tinto, V. (2000). Developing partnerships with academic affairs to enhance student learning. In M. J. Barr & M. K. Desler (Eds.), *The handbook of student affairs administration* (2nd ed., pp. 425–452). San Francisco: Jossey-Bass.

Entwistle, N. (2000). Promoting deep learning through teaching and assessment. In L. Suskie (Ed.), *Assessment to promote deep learning: Insights from AAHE's 2000 and 1999 assessment conferences* (pp. 9–19). Washington, DC: American Association for Higher Education.

Nelson, A. (2001). *Education and democracy: The meaning of Alexander Meiklejohn, 1872–1964.* Madison: University of Wisconsin Press.

The Higher Education Learning Community of Syracuse University

A Participant's Perspective

Maria J. Lopez

WHEN I was accepted into the Graduate School of Syracuse University, I viewed it as an experience I would go through alone. But my participation in the university's Higher Education Learning Community changed all that. What I discovered was a close-knit community of fellow learners who helped me to grow personally and academically in ways I could never have predicted.

The Learning Community: My Introduction and Preparation

I was first introduced to the Higher Education Learning Community on Graduate Assistantship Day. On this day, accepted students are given an opportunity to visit the institution, learn more about the program, and interview for possible assistantships. Upper-class students shared information about the learning community as well as brief anecdotes about their experiences. During the summer, I received newsletters that contained brief biographies of the students in our cohort, formal information about the program, an anecdote from a second-year student, and information about our mentors for the following year. Before we began the program, all participants were given a brief orientation by a faculty member and staff members who explained their expectations and provided detailed information about the courses we would take and how they were linked together.

Fortunately, I came to graduate school with an advantage. Unlike many of the other participants, I had recently attended Syracuse University for my undergraduate studies. I was already familiar with the student population and the institution's structure, pedagogies, values, and goals, because I had experienced them first-hand. I also had a prior familiarity with learning communities and the benefits they provide to students.

My First-Year Graduate Experience

I expected graduate study to consist of an extensive amount of coursework and personal isolation. However, during orientation, that expectation began to change. As a learning community, I learned, we would all take three classes together: Lab in Learning Communities (Lab in LC), Educational Research (ER), and Principles and Practices in Student Affairs (PPSA). These classes were connected by a fourth one-credit course: the Graduate Interest Group (GIG).

In Lab in LC, the staff explained, we were to learn the definition of a learning community and to explore why learning communities work or fail through literature and observations of learning communities. We would then apply the knowledge we gained by learning to assess learning communities. PPSA was an introductory course focusing on the field of student affairs, the goals and functions of student affairs, and how we could be better practitioners. In ER, we were to learn the differences between quantitative and qualitative research, what makes such methods valid, and how we could use each method to conduct research on college students. In GIG, we were asked to look at the connections between the literature and student experiences, as well as our own experiences as students and future professionals, and to consider how all of it might come together in student affairs practice.

How Did the Classes Connect?

The two classes most tied together were Lab in LC and PPSA. Much of the literature in these courses overlapped. Both courses began with a history of each and a review of the development of learning communities and student affairs as a profession. In these courses we learned that collaboration can occur within student affairs and in partnership with academic affairs to encourage student learning by creating a holistic environment. Learning communities are an example of this. PPSA showed us how departments can be involved with each other and Lab in LC showed how departments can work along with academic affairs.

ER gave us the opportunity to learn how to conduct qualitative and quantitative research in an educational setting and experience the challenges that come with doing research. In the quantitative section we learned how to critically analyze research for validity. We also had the opportunity to conduct qualitative interviews and compile a report of our findings. Learning how to gather information through qualitative research gave us the skills to assess learning communities as part of Lab in LC. Throughout the semester we observed learning communities by attending their classes and activities. We then shared our observations with the rest of the class. Along with the skills gained in doing qualitative research, these observations were helpful when conducting and analyzing focus groups for the various learning communities we observed. We were able to critically assess the learning communities and present recommendations for future practices.

GIG was the course that solidified the other courses. In GIG we discussed how the material was interconnected. During our first semester we used journals to reflect on our adjustment to graduate school and the course material. This gave us the opportunity to share our frustrations and challenges, critically analyze our experiences, and provide some feedback to the faculty about how we were experiencing the program. A few students in my cohort worked at other institutions, lived outside Syracuse, or were attending the program part time. GIG provided us with the opportunity to stay connected with members of the cohort who because of their part time status were not in some of the classes. GIG was also a chance for us to discuss professional ethics, analyze how our personalities impacted the group through the Myers-Briggs Type Inventory, and debrief the teambuilding ropes course we participated in earlier that academic year. In GIG, we were also given an opportunity to explore campus resources. We additionally used our time together to learn from the experiences of our peers.

How I Was Validated and Challenged

When I began graduate school I believed I was limited in my experiences because I had completed my undergraduate degree only four months prior and was attending the same institution for graduate study. As time progressed, I realized that these circumstances did not hinder me; rather they enhanced my graduate experiences. I was already familiar with Syracuse University and its various components. I was especially knowledgeable about student culture and how students experienced and navigated their education. Consequently, my peers began to see me as a resource. I was also encouraged by faculty to share my unique experiences and insider knowledge with my colleagues. This helped to build my confidence in my abilities and made me realize I had much to contribute. For the first time in my higher education tenure I felt validated in the classroom by my peers.

While they validated my experiences, my peers and instructors also challenged me to move beyond them to see how it all played out in the bigger picture. This was accomplished with the help of my peers, who shared their own practitioner stories and asked for critiques. As the semester progressed, discussions continued outside of the classroom, which was something I also had not experienced before. I was once again challenged by my peers, this time to think critically outside of the classroom.

How Does It All Come Together?

I believe the learning community played an integral role in giving all participants the skills to challenge each other intellectually inside and outside of the classroom. We were equipped with knowledge of the program's pedagogy and the teaching styles of the faculty. We also became aware of each other's learning styles and ways in which we worked in collaborative groups. All of this was a result of the Higher Education Learning Community. I also believe this learning community helped with my transition into graduate school. It not only connected the material and topics academically, but did so in a way that allowed us to use the knowledge from the literature and each other's experiences as students and practitioners to be better educators, so we might facilitate student success. This learning community also helped to create relationships with colleagues that made us dependent on each other for motivation and validation as well as advice on becoming better practitioners.

Personally, the learning community allowed me to see the bigger picture of student affairs. I quickly learned to value the multiple perspectives and experiences of my colleagues and faculty. I also learned that although I am new to the field now, my recent experiences as an undergraduate and student of color are equally important and as valued as those of my peers. The learning community gave me the skills to constructively critique and challenge my peers both in and out of the classroom. The learning community also taught me how to hold my peers accountable for their own education and for my education by sharing with them how much I valued their contributions and by continuously asking them for constructive feedback. My peers and I became interdependent, and to my understanding this is what much of the field of student affairs is like. My colleagues ultimately became a support system and a source of encouragement when work became challenging. Later I found out that I had done the same in return, for one peer in particular. This peer said, "If it weren't for you I would have been lost and would have left after my first semester." I believe that if this learning community had not existed, I would not have had the opportunity to learn so much from my peers.

Implementing the Program: Advice for Faculty

If faculty or staff members are interested in implementing this learning community model, I would recommend that they contact the participating students prior to starting the program. It would be helpful to have a formal letter letting students know that they will be members of a learning community, and informing them of the courses they will be taking. Just before the program begins, faculty or staff should send a newsletter to students with an introduction to the program by the chair or learning community faculty. The newsletter should also include a brief biography of each student entering the incoming cohort, as well as a reflection piece from a prior student on the first-year experience. These elements helped me prepare to meet my future colleagues and see what their interests were. Just before students arrive, faculty and staff should send specific orientation materials to students regarding places to eat, community resources on and off campus, and institutional events that the students could participate in. This is an effective way for future students to become familiar with the campus community prior to arrival.

I believe an important part of my learning community experience was the opportunity to work in groups. Working in smaller groups that varied throughout the academic year provided me with the chance to hear multiple, diverse perspectives, to critique and accept criticism, to create support networks for different needs, and eventually to learn how to work with a variety of people, making me more aware of others' learning styles and multiple ways to communicate information.

One factor that played an important role was the observation and assessment of other learning communities. In Lab in LC we observed and evaluated learning communities at Syracuse University and the State University of New York College of Environmental Science and Forestry. We eventually conducted focus groups to assess these same learning communities. Participating in these activities and reading the literature allowed me to be cognizant of what I should be learning in my own learning community as well as of ways to enhance my own experience and get the most out of the learning community.

My participation in this learning community offered me the chance to evaluate myself, my peers, and the faculty in a shared way. In Lab in LC we provided written evaluations of our peers' participation. We also had group evaluations regarding our own participation in the group. That data was then collectively shared with the group, along with comments from the faculty. Last, we shared with the faculty our understanding of the information we were learning. We also had discussions that focused on ways to communicate with each other to make the classroom effective.

In conclusion, I recommend that faculty make students aware of their availability outside of class and that they remain open to feedback. It is important to provide a chance for students to share concerns and discuss their experiences. I found the staff of my learning community to be open to what I had to say and how I experienced the program. For me, this form of validation was just as important as validation from my peers.

Through the Looking Glass of Undergraduate Learning Communities
(And What the Graduate Student Finds)

Chris Calvert-Minor

IN *Through the Looking Glass and What Alice Found There* (1872), author Lewis Carroll writes of a young girl, Alice, standing in front of a mirror and wondering what might be present in the "looking glass house," that is, the house she sees reflected in the looking glass. Her interest is to know whether the warming fire in the room she just came from, not quite visible in the reflection of the mirror, is also there in the looking glass house. With curiosity and a heavy dose of fantasy, Alice slips through the looking glass plane, emerges on the other side, and starts exploring that house, where she does indeed find the fire that warms the house.

Using this scene as a metaphor, consider a graduate student walking up to the looking glass of *undergraduate learning communities* (ULCs), a mirror that reflects the basic constitution of ULCs and shows how other learning communities compare. The graduate student peers into the looking glass with her own graduate community and education in mind. What does she see? How are they similar or dissimilar? After a moment, the graduate student steps through the looking glass and appears on the other side. What does she find as she explores the house? Like the initially unseen fire Alice finds that warms the house, is there something that warms the life of ULCs, something that, though not immediately apparent, sparks their success—something that the graduate student can learn from?

The metaphor of the ULC looking glass functions both to show the similarities and dissimilarities between ULCs and graduate communities and to act as a lens to pinpoint what graduate communities must do to match the success of ULCs. This essay will (1) offer a stance on the general, current state of graduate education, (2) address how guiding assumptions and attitudes in graduate education need to change, and (3) propose what graduate students, as future faculty, should bring to whatever teaching context they find themselves in. Ultimately, this is a call to improve graduate education as well as the education graduate students impart to others.

In the Reflection of the Looking Glass

Learning communities generally exist as formal programs for undergraduates and not as focal points of learning for graduate students. The research literature about universities with established learning communities refers almost exclusively to undergraduates. Many graduate students shrug their shoulders in ignorance when asked for their impressions of learning communities because they have such limited exposure to those kinds of programs. However, it is now time to rethink this response; graduate students often overlook the fact that they are immersed within learning communities in their own departments.

Let us first consider what a ULC is in general terms. Many competing definitions and models on the constitution of ULCs exist, but Ruth Federman Stein and Vincent Tinto summarize it best. Stein (2004) distills the primary motivation for ULCs as the creation of an intellectually stimulating environment that brings together students and faculty to produce better learning. Tinto (2000) characterizes their basic form as the co-enrollment of students in various distributions of courses. Whether the students in a ULC also live in a common residence or have additional responsibilities such as community service, the structural heart is common classes. Participating students take the same block of classes together, learning from their familiarity with each other as well as from their instructors. According to Tinto, the goal is the effective production of shared knowledge, shared knowing, and shared responsibility. *Shared knowledge* results from using the same materials, advancing the same themes, and engendering the same experiences with a group of students in hopes of encouraging higher levels of intellectual complexity. *Shared knowing* occurs by virtue of the diversity of participants and their inclusion in the construction of knowledge together. Getting to know each other and dealing with varying perspectives helps students achieve differential collective learning. *Shared responsibility* is the result of col-laboration and mutual reliance on one another for the successful completion of projects.

As the graduate student peers into the looking glass of ULCs, she notices that this fits her graduate education too. Graduate students also participate in similar learning environments that one might call *graduate learning com-munities* (GLCs), which are comprised of fellow graduate students and faculty within their own departments. Life within these departments generally consists of the same group of graduate students taking the same block of classes together, maybe also working together as TAs, and milling around the graduate student lounge talking about classes and research. This structure fits well with Stein's motivational definition of a learning community and, especially, with the more concrete definition that Tinto offers. Shared knowledge and shared knowing are functions of taking the same classes together and having to interact with one another. Likewise, shared responsibility occurs whenever collaborative efforts are required. Such collaborative efforts include seminar presentations, problem sets, research projects, and TA-related activities. Most graduate students are, then, already part of a GLC similar in basic structure to ULCs.

However, there is an important dissimilarity between ULCs and GLCs. Those ULCs that focus more on improving education than just on retaining students encourage learning through *liberal education*, an approach to education that rigorously promotes a high level of critical reflection, active engagement, and responsible understanding of oneself in the world. This has been, in fact, the historical motivation behind learning communities (Smith, 2003). Therefore, great care is put into fending off the ultra-pragmatic approach common in today's universities—particularly research institutions—whereby education serves only as a means to an end (e.g., getting into graduate school or landing a job). The sentiment is that ULCs should function not only as instruments in students' career paths, but also as ends in themselves, by facilitating critical thinking and reflection to equip students with the skills necessary to navigate and succeed in their academic and co-curricular experiences. Unfortunately, liberal education is rarely present in GLCs. Graduate education generally sacrifices all the breadth of a liberal education for the depth of one's disciplinary courses and particular research area. "Specialization" is the name of the game, despite Catharine Stimpson's (2004) warning that this exclusivity makes graduate discourse and thought myopic. Thus, graduate education needs to change. Breadth and depth need not be mutually exclusive, indeed they must not be if graduate education is to foster a critical sense of social responsibility.

As future faculty and professionals, graduate students will be given the space to make a great impact on those around them. Whether they are in the classroom, the lab, the studio, or the office, their education and their perspectives will be valued and given serious weight in issues involving curricula, procedures, projects, and policies. To help cultivate a sense of social responsibility so that graduate students make reflective, responsible choices, graduate education needs to incorporate liberal education. As future faculty, graduate students need to understand on *whom* they will have an impact, *why* they should have an impact on them, and with *what* tools they should make that impact. These are vital questions that, when asked and reflected upon, will deepen the graduate student's education and sense of social responsibility. The concrete aspects of graduate education are, of course, important; however, incorporating more elements of a liberal education into the graduate experience would only enrich graduate education. Many ULCs provide the space for this kind of discourse, while most GLCs need to catch up.

Through the Lens of the Looking Glass

The success of ULCs is well documented. Tinto's research shows that ULC students more actively engage their coursework inside the classroom while also forming "self-supporting" groups that encourage them to learn better outside the classroom (2000); the students bond both socially and intellect- tually. The overall effect is that these students seem to experience a higher quality of education than students outside of the learning communities. Likewise, testimony from students who participate certainly provides evidence that ULCs enjoy a great measure of success. But this cannot be simply because there is a structure in place that engenders these positive effects. At most, the ULC structure raises the possibility of success, it does not assure the actuality.

There is a difference between setting up the conditions for something to happen and the happening itself. One can, for example, set up the conditions for a successful dinner—the table is set, the food is well prepared and ready, and the guests are all sitting at the table—but, though all the elements are structurally present, the dinner is not successful until the guests begin eating and enjoying the food. In the same way, even if all the conditions exist for a successful ULC, success is not guaranteed. To discover what actualizes the success of ULCs, one must go through the looking glass and search for their warming fire.

Like Alice in her escapades, the graduate student slips through the looking glass of ULCs, begins exploring its house, and discovers that what lies behind the structure of ULCs is that those who participate in them, both students and faculty alike, have the *appropriate guiding assumptions and attitudes* that facilitate success. They understand the purpose, goals, and work required of ULCs. They desire what ULCs offer and want to contribute to their success. Students who enter into ULCs are often those who are eager to learn in communal contexts and who desire the deeper, more reflective understandings of a liberal education. Likewise, faculty members who volunteer their time and resources to ULCs generally want to facilitate a more liberal, more construc- tive education. They understand the value of collaborative work for their own betterment and for the betterment of the students. If ULCs existed in structure only, and these guiding assumptions and attitudes were absent, ULCs would surely fail—for these subjective factors are the components that spark and fuel the ULC fire. Co-enrollment and block distributions of courses are not enough to ensure ULC success, though certainly these structural elements are integral. Yet, when the general ULC structure is combined with the appropriate assumptions and attitudes necessary to learn and teach in the spirit of liberal education, success is almost guaranteed. (It is, then, little wonder that the research on ULCs is positive—ULCs tend to attract those who have the appropriate assumptions and attitudes; only those who want more of a liberal education and a communal context sign up. As long as ULCs remain on a volunteer basis, they are ready-made for success.)

So the question remains: What can the graduate student learn from the ULC fire? First, if GLCs are to move closer to liberal education, all involved (students, faculty, and administration) must adopt the appropriate assumptions and attitudes. They must have a clear understanding of what needs to be done to integrate liberal education and they must desire it. This might seem an overwhelming task—one that would require many graduate departments to go through a paradigm shift, even a change of academic culture. Many departments are neither equipped nor philosophically directed to embrace liberal education. They are, instead, rooted in academic competition and individual achievement, which detracts from the spirit of liberal education (Hall, 2006). Collaborative efforts do exist, but, without the appropriate support necessary for them to grow in such a pervasively competitive atmosphere, they are few in number. In general, the intense competition of GLCs is an *intra*departmental phenomenon, but it also exists *inter*departmentally, making joint efforts to encourage liberal education difficult. Only when GLCs begin adopting the appropriate guiding assumptions and attitudes for a liberal education can they start to enjoy the kind of success witnessed in ULCs.

Second, since attitudes play a primary role, those graduate students who desire a more liberal education now and cannot find it within their current GLCs can seek out other like-minded graduate students and construct *makeshift* GLCs. This could be difficult given the amount of time graduate students must dedicate to departmental degree requirements, but their focus could be kept simple. Such GLCs could consist of self-supporting groups of students who critically address their education and responsibilities in the context of a shared structure to help direct and focus them. Shared structures could include courses taken together across disciplines and discussed reflectively in light of liberal education, but they could grow to include talks, seminars, and committees that facilitate critical thinking and reflection.

Makeshift GLCs may already exist at some schools. For example, the Graduate School at Syracuse University specializes in creating opportunities ripe for these kinds of GLCs. The Graduate School annually appoints 24 experienced TAs to organize and conduct an orientation for new TAs at the start of the academic year. In their preparation and during the orientations, these TAs spend quite a few hours discussing and reflecting on teaching techniques, responsibilities, philosophies, and issues of diversity among themselves and in the small groups of new TAs they lead. In other words, they spend a great deal of time discussing many of the central elements of a graduate student liberal education. These are makeshift GLCs.

Syracuse University offers another opportunity in the form of committees for which the Graduate School recruits volunteers. For instance, one committee of graduate students formed during the spring semester of 2005 with the specific purpose of discussing the issue of liberal education for graduate students. Like participants in successful ULCs, these ten students from diverse backgrounds spent their time together critically thinking beyond their own departments and their own experiences.

Last, and perhaps most applicable to any school, makeshift GLCs have cropped up at Syracuse University due to shared interests and goals among graduate students. These include interdisciplinary collaborations to develop education manuals, working dissertation support groups, and graduate student get-togethers that turn into critical discussions of their education and social responsibility. Makeshift GLCs can start from any shared interest or goal; the question is whether the individual graduate students are willing to take the initiative, especially those whose departments do not facilitate a GLC.

Building and Fueling the Fire

ULCs are doing something right. They are fostering a liberal education that is foundational for the undergraduate experience. GLCs need to do the same for the graduate experience. Not all graduate students will teach in universities upon earning degrees, but graduate departments are the training ground for those who desire to do so. As future faculty, graduate students must be even more adept at critical thinking and at promoting liberal education than the students they will eventually guide. For this to work, graduate students, faculty, and administration alike must begin to hold the same kinds of assumptions and attitudes that permeate ULCs; GLCs must begin to build the metaphorical fire in the looking glass house, to stoke and fuel it until it warms the GLCs with the ideals that nurture liberal education. Only then can the values that graduate students receive from that education be recycled into the values of their future teaching and the values that guide their students.

References

Carroll, L. (1872). *Through the looking glass and what Alice found there.* London: Macmillan.

Hall, D. E. (2006, January 4). Collegiality and graduate school training. *Inside Higher Ed.* Retrieved October 8, 2009, from http://insidehighered.com/workplace/2006/01/04/hall#

Smith, B. L. (2003). Learning communities and liberal education. *Academe, 89*(1), 14–18.

Stein, R. F. (2004). Learning communities: An overview. In S. N. Hurd & R. F. Stein (Eds.), *Building and sustaining learning communities: The Syracuse University experience* (pp. 3–18). Bolton, MA: Anker.

Stimpson, C. R. (2004). Reclaiming the mission of graduate education. *Chronicle of Higher Education, 50*(41), B6–B8.

Tinto, V. (2000). Learning better together: The impact of learning communities on student success. *Journal of Institutional Research in Australasia, 9* (1), 48–53.

The Mary Ann Shaw Center for Public and Community Service
Lessons Learned

Elizabeth Occhino and Jennifer Kellington

The excellence of education can well be measured in this world by our ability and willingness not to sit passively and comfortably with our separateness and our habits of mind, but instead to actively engage with people and ideas, however hard this work turns out to be.... We want Syracuse students to feel they have been given real opportunities in settings where those with diverse interests and backgrounds can find ways to engage each other.
—Nancy Cantor, "Scholarship in Action: Building the Creative Campus"

IN 1994, Syracuse University (SU) launched an engagement initiative with the goal of encouraging and supporting faculty and staff in their efforts to work together for intellectual, ethical, professional, and personal development through reciprocal learning in partnership with the community. The centerpiece of this effort was the Mary Ann Shaw Center for Public and Community Service (CPCS), which implemented a residential Service Learning Community (SLC) from 2001 to 2005, currently facilitates more than thirty community-based service-learning courses, and manages more than 200 SU Literacy Corps tutors as part of the university's America Reads program. The center also allows students to develop leadership skills through the following community-based service-learning programs: the Literacy Corps Council, Balancing the Books, First Book–Syracuse University, the CPCS Leadership Intern Program, and the Syracuse University Volunteer Organization. With CPCS as a valuable resource, the practice of integrating community-based learning into both curricular and co-curricular experiences throughout campus continues to grow, with more than 5,000 participants each academic year.

CPCS works with individuals and departments from across campus, but its primary focus is to assist faculty with developing credit-bearing, community-based service learning courses for both undergraduate and graduate students. Hence, CPCS most closely associates its practices with Robert G. Bringle and Julie A. Hatcher's definition of service learning as

> a course-based, credit-bearing educational experience in which students (a) participate in an organized service activity that meets identified community needs and (b) reflect on the service activity in such a way as to gain further understanding of course content, a broader appreciation of the discipline, and an enhanced sense of civic responsibility. (1995, p. 112)

Community-based service learning provides equal benefits and foci for the recipients, the community-based organizations, the providers, and the students. All service experiences provide students the opportunity to give back to the community. Service learning, however, is unique when compared to other forms of experiential education, due to its "intention to equally benefit the provider and the recipient of the service as well as to ensure equal focus on both service being provided and the learning that is occurring" (Furco, 1996, p. 5). This chapter highlights CPCS's experience with its Service Learning Community and gives recommendations for incorporating service within learning communities.

A New Concept in Learning Communities

In 2001, CPCS responded to growing interest by students and faculty to engage in more sophisticated community-based service learning experiences by partnering with the Office of Residence Life (ORL) and the Office of Learning Communities (OLC) to develop a residential Service Learning Community for juniors and seniors. CPCS has implemented a residential SLC each academic year since, continuously making changes to accommodate student and faculty interests. The interdisciplinary nature of the consecutive offerings of CPCS's SLC allowed participants to develop individual interests and reflect on their personal experiences while building a sense of civic responsibility in both the classroom and the residence hall, creating a true living-learning community.

Though the format of the SLC has changed significantly since its initial offering, the following learning outcomes, defined in 2001, continued to provide the framework for all subsequent SLC offerings (Flynn & Riemer, 2004, 155–156):

- develop a spirit of partnership with the community;
- understand the nonprofit sector while exploring roles and responsibility as citizens;
- develop an awareness of larger societal issues and how local

resources are allocated to them;

- develop an awareness and understanding of diversity as well as prejudices, stereotypes, and different realities.

Success and Growth

While service learning impacts the development and learning of college students, it can, at the same time, increase student retention through student and faculty interactions and a sense of community on campus. On large college or university campuses, in particular, students may feel overwhelmed because of the size. "Service learning can provide the context for reducing this sense of isolation in a way that gives meaning to the student's life" (Eyler & Giles, 1999, p. 49). SU's unique geographic position—high on a hill overlooking the city—creates an invisible barrier between campus and certain sections of the city of Syracuse. This situation tends to create a feeling of isolation among students in relation to the rest of the community. In the experience of CPCS, students who have participated in community-based service learning often comment on how the personal connections they made through their service learning experiences have resulted in a deeper sense of connectedness to the city.

Service learning can impact students in different ways depending on their backgrounds, their experiences prior to coming to campus, and the amount of time faculty dedicate to helping students process their current service experiences. The effectiveness of the faculty, reflection pieces, student–faculty interaction, and quality of the service learning experience also are factors (Eyler & Giles, 1999).

Thomas Ehrlich, former president of Indiana University and a proponent of service learning, supports John Dewey's pragmatic approach to learning. According to Ehrlich,

> Dewey believed that individuals should not be trained for narrow professions alone but for life, and that learning in the classroom and in practical arenas should constantly interact—lest we be unable to learn from our experiences or link those experiences to our intellectual inquiries. (Ehrlich & Frey, 1995, pp. 88–89)

The act of combining service with other forms of experiential learning, such as learning communities, can have a powerful effect on student learning. "Learning communities provide an intellectual environment that fosters student voice and active engagement with complex, capacious problems and ideas. Service learning applies this knowledge in service to broader community needs" (Leavitt & Oates, 2003, p. 5). Reflection, an essential component of service learning pedagogy, is "the link that ties student experience in the community to academic learning" (Eyler & Giles, 1999, p. 171). This provides students the opportunity to process their service experiences in terms of their course content. Through intellectual discourse students develop a deeper understanding of their educational experiences.

Since the initiative was introduced at SU, the number of learning communities that incorporate some level of service has significantly increased. This blend has proved to be an effective and innovative approach to achieving the university's mission of connecting campus and community. The personal connections students describe as a result of their off-campus service experiences are similar to those they forge on campus within their learning communities.

Though many faculty and staff members integrate service to support the theme of their learning communities, the level of engagement can fall at various levels on the continuum between community service and community-based service learning. As shown in Figure 1, community service results in a greater benefit for the recipient, typically a community-based organization.

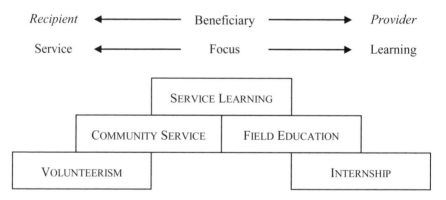

FIGURE 1. Types of service programs arrayed along two continua.
Source: Furco, 1996, p. 3.

Community service alone can, however, lead to a service learning experience when "students begin to engage in formal intellectual discourse around the various issues relevant to the cause" (Furco, 1996, p. 4). For example, students who begin their community service at a homeless shelter may start to understand hunger as a global issue and reflect on this experience by registering for a community-based service learning course the following semester.

Designing a learning community with a service component can be a challenging yet innovative approach to engaging students both on and off campus. Things to consider before deciding on a learning community format are learning outcomes, faculty interest, relationships with community partners, and scheduling.

Need for Flexibility

CPCS has experimented with a combination of models, as described by Lynn H. Leavitt and Karen K. Oates (2003), to achieve the desired outcomes while also responding to faculty and student interests. One of the greatest lessons those involved with CPCS have learned while integrating service learning into learning communities in recent years is that flexibility is crucial for success. Requirements and offerings have evolved to meet the program's changed needs. For example:

- When the program was launched in 2001, juniors and seniors registered for the one-credit Seminar in Service Learning and an additional one-to-three-credit service-learning course while also completing 35 hours of individual service of their choice.
- In 2004, the program changed. First-year students registered for one of several three-credit service-learning courses, completed 20 hours of individual service, attended a community tour, and participated in four skills-building workshops.
- In 2005, first-year participating students registered for one section of a three-credit introductory writing course, completed 20 hours of individual service, attended a community tour, and participated in two group service activities.

Keys to Success

Developing successful community-based service-learning courses presents faculty with similar challenges to those encountered when creating learning communities. Creating new endeavors, programs, or projects that involve academics requires faculty whose scholarly interests will be well served by the innovative pedagogy, since there is always a significant increase in time spent on developing new academic initiatives. This is especially true when working with off-campus community partners. Over the years, CPCS has learned many valuable lessons from the multiple SLC offerings. For instance, a community-based service-learning course related to a specific content area is much more effective than a stand-alone community-based service-learning course.

In order to create successful service-learning experiences, CPCS partici-pants have learned that it is necessary to allow adequate time for planning by selecting a learning community coordinating team that includes faculty and community partners. Ideally, community partners should be asked to partici-pate in every aspect of the process, perhaps even remaining involved as active participants in the learning process. At the lowest level of involvement, faculty and staff should meet with community partners on a regular basis to gain community feedback, while incorporating opportunities for feedback and encouraging open communication throughout the process. Most importantly, successfully integrating service learning into learning communities relies heavily on utilizing campus service centers or experienced service-learning faculty for support in the planning, implementation, and assessment phases. Despite new challenges each semester, there is one constant: students who continue to be motivated by the experience will become leaders both within their peer group and in the larger Syracuse community. Because of this, CPCS continues to build on existing partnerships and promote learning opportunities through community-based service learning.

References

Bringle, R. G., & Hatcher, J. A. (1995). A service-learning curriculum for faculty. *Michigan Journal of Community Service Learning, 2,* 112–122.

Ehrlich, T., & Frey, J. (1995). *The courage to inquire: Ideals and realities in higher education.* Indianapolis: Indiana University Press.

Eyler, J., & Giles, D. (1999). *Where's the learning in service learning?* San Francisco: Jossey-Bass.

Flynn, L., & Riemer, S. (2004). Constructing concentric communities. In S. N. Hurd & R. F. Stein (Eds.), *Building and sustaining learning communities: The Syracuse University experience* (pp. 153–67). Bolton, MA: Anker.

Furco, A. (1996). Service-learning: A balanced approach to experiential education. In B. Taylor (Ed.), *Expanding boundaries: Serving and learning* (pp. 2–6). Washington, DC: Corporation for National Service.

Leavitt, L. H., & Oates, K. K. (2003). *Service-learning and learning communities: Tools for integration and assessment.* Washington, DC: Association of American Colleges and Universities.

Mentoring and the Gateway Learning Community
The Importance of Mentoring in Providing Access to Social Capital

Larry Thomas and Nicole Zervas Adsitt

RESEARCH has shown that high-achieving college students from under-resourced and marginalized populations often feel disconnected from social networks within institutions of higher education. Until recently, many theorists viewed this disconnect through the lens of deficit theory, particularly when examining cultural and social capital. In fact, the disconnect evidences the idea that cultural capital "refers to an accumulation of specific forms of knowledge, skills and abilities that are *valued* by privileged groups in society" (Yosso, 2005, p. 70). Certain values remain privileged within institutions of higher education, therefore making the capital or sociocultural wealth that under-graduates bring with them to college invisible (Banks, 2007; Yosso, 2005). Many programs designed to address educational inequality are crafted and operationalized using deficit frameworks, thus indirectly reinforcing institu-tionalized inequity.

To strategically address this issue, the Collegiate Science and Technology Entry Program (CSTEP) at Syracuse University established the Gateway Learning Community, a residential program that supports students as they prepare for entry into medical school and pre-health careers. The formal and informal mentoring relationships that participating undergraduates develop with influential faculty members and administrators are at the heart of the program's success. Since the program's inception in 2004, mentors have both enhanced intellectual capital and brokered social and cultural capital for participants in Gateway. Mentors augment the sociocultural wealth of high-achieving students while also helping them to think critically and strategically about how dominant capital operates in the college setting and to navigate within this framework.

Faculty and students engaged in Gateway benefit from the reciprocity of social networking across pre-health disciplines. An example of such an exchange involves student participation in research. Faculty members receive research assistance from high-achieving undergraduate students, while the students become better prepared for graduate-level research and education through the mentoring relationship. In essence, Gateway acts as a conduit for faculty seeking the synergistic experience necessary for tenure, as well as for obtaining sponsorship for research.

The Community

In the transition from college to the "real" world, undergraduates of color are often forced to embrace the social values and norms of the majority. This can be especially daunting, as many of today's college students of color come from historically underresourced communities where social networks have eroded as a result of systemic isolation. Robert Putnam (2000) explains:

> The parts of the United States where social trust and other forms of social capital are lowest today are in places where slavery and racialist policy were most entrenched historically. The civil rights movement was, in part, aimed at destroying certain exclusive, non-bridging forms of social capital—racially homogeneous schools, neighborhoods, and so forth. The deeper question was what was to follow, and in some sense this question remains as high on the national agenda at the beginning of the twenty-first century as it was at the beginning of the twentieth. (p. 362)

With that issue in mind, the Gateway Learning Community sought to provide pre-health students with "highly valued and scarce resources" through increased faculty and staff interactions (Berger, 2000, p. 98).

Through the integration of academic, social, and residential life, Gateway prepares undergraduates for health careers, global citizenship, and lifelong achievement. Scholars reside in a community populated mostly by graduate and law students—the most appropriate role models for Gateway residents preparing to enter graduate or professional school. In total, eleven staff members, ten faculty, and five graduate students collaborate to implement curricular, co-curricular, and extracurricular experiences. This connection to faculty and staff, as well as their networks, synthesizes core competencies learned in the classroom with the social and cultural contexts of education, thus bridging the gaps between human, social, and cultural capital.

Mentoring

Dawn Wallace, Ron Abel, and Becky Ropers-Huilman (2000) have studied methods of breaking down traditional barriers through undergraduate mentoring. They found that very little research had been conducted on formal mentoring programs, especially those involving underrepresented populations. However, informal mentoring relationships do not typically develop in ways that benefit all students. Consequently, programs that create opportunities for mentoring may serve as a conduit for student success, particularly for under-represented students (Wallace et al., 2000). Similar research suggests that mentoring relationships established by faculty and staff contribute to the persistence and retention of underrepresented students (Kobrak, 1992).

Students of color often feel unprepared for the racial, cultural, and political aspects of the workplace upon graduation. Therefore, Gateway aims to ensure that residents not only learn how to make sense of social and cultural capital themselves, but also know how to share it within their social networks (Berger, 2000). To that end, CSTEP recruited and selected faculty, staff, and graduate student mentors who had influence, knowledge, and contacts that would support the Gateway students. The process bears a resemblance to the practice described in Elijah Anderson's study of racial identities in the corporate world (2001). Of all the individuals asked to participate in Gateway, only those faculty, staff, and graduate students "who, because of upbringing, education, or general life experiences, have developed a deeply sympathetic or empathetic orientation toward people" of socially disadvantaged background were selected as mentors (Anderson, 2001, p. 424).

While a very intentional part of Gateway's design involved initiating student–faculty connections, this mentoring infrastructure was not transparent to the students. Consistent with Wallace et al.'s (2000) findings, the students in the Gateway Learning Community had an unclear understanding of mentoring relationships. They did not recognize their own experiences as mentoring, though they did see the value of having a mentor. For example, in a focus group, one resident said, "No matter how old you are, you need a mentor." Yet none of the residents felt that they had a mentor, or felt comfortable seeking out a mentor. On the other hand, they described several examples of mentoring experiences and how aspects of cultural and social capital were made visible to them through these experiences. One Gateway scholar described meeting a faculty member she would not have met outside the community and how this meeting created new opportunities through intentional connections and the encouragement of her established goals. Thus, residents often benefited from mentoring relationships without recognizing them as such.

Also important in fostering student success were the frequent social events that provided opportunities for Gateway residents to connect with faculty or graduate students in a variety of settings. Several dinners were held at the homes of faculty fellows, who not only introduced the students to faculty and staff members but also assisted them in establishing an inclusive faculty/staff network on campus. These events often alleviated the awkwardness that some students experience when interacting with faculty and staff. For example, a student in a 2005 focus group expressed her discomfort in approaching faculty and staff members for guidance by asking, "When you see someone you admire, how do you go about saying, 'Can we meet up sometime and maybe talk?' You know, that's awkward." For many residents, attending a networking social at a faculty member's home creates a space where students can learn how to navigate the complex boundaries between faculty and students. Moreover, it provides a comfortable, outside-of-the-classroom environment where students can socialize with their peers as well as their professors. As expected, many of the social barriers of the classroom, or the students' perceptions of barriers, are removed.

Wallace et al. state that "although students in our study indicated a desire for a faculty mentor, these relationships were simply not forming spontaneously. The complete absence of informal faculty mentoring relationships indicated a strong need for other institutional personnel to make connections with students" (2000, p. 13). The Gateway Learning Community provided experiences that allowed these intentional connections to develop.

Other Benefits of Faculty Involvement

Faculty involvement elicits critical insight and feedback that helps further strengthen the learning community experience for students, thus promoting student success. For example, one faculty fellow thought that helping students develop their writing skills would be essential to their transition to graduate/ professional school or a professional work setting. Therefore, we incorporated an upper-level writing course into the program. This proved particularly challenging since students had only a few courses remaining before graduation and did not know how to fit a required course into their schedules. As expected, not all of our residents were receptive to the idea. However, while it was a difficult decision to make as a planning team, the Gateway steering committee decided it was in the students' best interest to move forward with the course and enlisted a writing instructor willing to meet with the residents to gather ideas for course design. This flexibility and eagerness to engage residents is characteristic of the ways that barriers are deconstructed in a learning community. In the end, the course was well received. One Gateway scholar declared that she planned to write a senior thesis because of the writing course.

Implications

Genuine relationships with faculty, staff, graduate students, and peers early in students' academic careers spur their holistic development. This process enhances the understanding of how intellectual, social, and cultural capital works within institutions, which then has "a strong positive impact on college completion, graduate education, and educational attainment" (Berger, 2000). The Gateway Learning Community makes important contributions to the personal growth of Syracuse University's scholars and provides them with long-term mentoring in their academic, personal, and professional lives.

The key objectives for educators include student learning and success. For those of us involved, the experience of creating the Gateway Learning Community has changed our thinking about the importance of learning environments in shaping learning outcomes. First, we have come to understand how the context of learning communities is critical to creating intentional mentoring opportunities. Further, cultivating a small, cohesive community has proved to increase undergraduate students' opportunities for connections with faculty, staff, graduate students, and peers. In turn, this type of involvement provides faculty with the type of synergistic experience that allows for professional development as well as the promotion of student success. By taking advantage of these different opportunities within learning communities, faculty support successful learning environments in significant ways. Overall, we have experienced a transformation—one that has allowed our faculty and graduate mentors to better understand and support students as they navigate their path to success.

It is clear that we need to learn more about how to create intentional learning environments for our undergraduates, particularly underrepresented students in the academy. Awareness of how networks are formed in academia constitutes crucial knowledge, yet this awareness is not readily available to all students. As educators, we need to be cognizant of the many complex issues that surround learning and be willing to examine nontraditional pedagogical methods. Learning to move beyond formal pathways and find means to intentionally connect with students on an informal basis is imperative for future faculty. It is precisely this type of transformative teaching, advising, and mentoring that can be found in a variety of learning community contexts.

References

Anderson, E. (2001). The social situation of the black executive: Black and white identities in the corporate world. In E. Anderson & D. Massey (Eds.), *Problem of the century: Racial stratification in the United States* (pp. 405–436). New York: Russell Sage Foundation.

Banks, C. A. (2007). This is how we do it! Black women undergraduates, cultural capital and college success—reworking discourse (Doctoral dissertation, Syracuse University, 2006). *Dissertation Abstracts International, 67* (11). (UMI No. 3241847)

Berger, J. B. (2000). Optimizing capital, social reproduction, and under-graduate persistence: A sociological perspective. In J. M. Braxton (Ed.), *Reworking the student departure puzzle* (pp. 95–126). Nashville, TN: Vanderbilt University Press.

Kobrak, P. (1992). Black student retention in predominately white regional universities: The politics of faculty involvement. *Journal of Negro Education, 61*(4), 509–530.

Putnam, R. D. (2000). *Bowling alone: The collapse and revival of American community.* New York: Touchstone.

Wallace, D., Abel, R., & Ropers-Huilman, B. (2000). Clearing a path for success: Deconstructing borders through undergraduate mentoring. *Review of Higher Education, 24*(1), 87–102.

Yosso, T. J. (2005). Whose culture has capital? A critical race theory discussion of community cultural wealth. *Race Ethnicity and Education, 8*(1), 69–91.

Institutional Pedagogies
Exploring Two Learning Community Programs

Jennah K. Jones and Joshua D. Lawrie

ACCORDING to theorist Richard Stimpson (1994), educational leaders generally strive to ensure that out-of-class experiences are thoughtfully developed and implemented. Many staff members of university residence life offices view themselves as educational leaders. As part of their jobs, residence life staff members often partner with faculty to strengthen and promote student learning within their halls (Schroeder & Mable, 1994). Learning communities, which are often based in residence halls and work to improve the education of students (Inkelas & Weisman, 2003), are one result of such partnerships. Though programs nationwide share similar pedagogical goals, their implementation varies greatly by institution. A close study of learning communities at two universities—Syracuse University in upstate New York and Ball State University in Muncie, Indiana—from the perspective of graduate student staff members shows how programs that are drastically different in structure can share similar educational success.

Syracuse University: The Leaders Emerging and Developing Program

Syracuse University offers students a unique opportunity to enhance learning through the coupled efforts of academic and student affairs. These two divisions collaborate to provide themed residential learning communities in which students sharing similar academic or co-curricular interests live together on a residence hall floor. Syracuse University also has curricular learning communities in which students not only live on the same floor but enroll in a set of linked classes. The professors of the linked classes meet with each other and with the student affairs professionals from the residence halls to discuss their students' progress and the learning process. This teaching-learning strategy is intended to enhance learning and understanding of course material. The arrangement ensures that participating students have a shared vision and collectively become a learning organization (Senge, 1990).

Student learning is at the core of Syracuse University's teaching philosophy regarding learning communities. Many learning community classes subscribe to the Learning Paradigm (Barr & Tagg, 1995), which focuses on student learning with particular emphasis on intention and environment. It is a holistic approach in which students co-create knowledge rather than absorbing it strictly through the lectures of instructors. Faculty and staff all play influential roles in the students' learning process (Barr & Tagg, 1995).

Jennah Jones worked with one particular program at Syracuse University, the Leaders Emerging and Developing (LEAD) learning community, in the fall semester of 2005. As a student affairs professional living and working in the hall where the LEAD learning community is housed, she played several different roles. Her interactions were both intentional and influential in her students' learning processes; she interacted with them on a daily basis, taught them in a leadership course, and advised them in their community council (hall government) efforts. Talking with learning community students one-on-one helped Jones become acquainted with the students personally, and helped her understand what they comprehended from their classes. These positive interactions were beneficial later in the classroom setting. Following are Jones's reflections on her experience:

> The LEAD learning community is a thematic learning community and not tied to an academic program, but the assistant director of residence life and I decided it needed an academic component. To that end, we co-taught a section of Public Affairs (PAF) 121: Growth Opportunities and Leadership Development for the LEAD students. This is a one-credit leadership studies course taught in two-hour class sessions over a six-week period. As instructors, we valued the experiential learning process in which students transfer outcomes from their PAF 121 course to the residential living environment. Educators rely on such methods to motivate students, increase their cognitive development, and create meaningful learning experiences (McKeachie, 1994).
>
> To enhance the experiential learning process, we based our curriculum on the Social Change Model of Leadership Development (Higher Education Research Institute, 1996). We explained this leadership model to our students and then watched as they created knowledge on the subject. They were empowered to demonstrate how they understood the theory through group projects and reflections, as suggested by Robert Barr and John Tagg (1995). Each week, we asked our students to write journal entries about experiences on the residential floor that demonstrated aspects of the Social Change Model. One of the important factors predicting student success,

learning, and development is the peer group (Astin, 1993). As student affairs professionals in the classroom, we were able to incorporate student development theories to enhance student learning. We assigned group projects that required students to prepare assignments together outside of the classroom. This task was not difficult because their residential structure allowed easy access to each other. We also used experiential strategies in their learning pedagogy for a more holistic education (Barr & Tagg, 1995). For example, one major assignment encouraged students to participate in a student organization for at least twenty hours and explain how that experience helped them to grow as leaders. Many of the students completed their hours through the community council, so I was able to see how they made connections between classroom and practical leadership experiences. This strategy created an environment in which students learned from their experiences rather than from instructors' lectures. The LEAD Learning Community section of PAF 121 philosophically reflected a learning paradigm in which the "mission is not instruction but rather that of producing learning with every student by whatever means works best" (Barr & Tagg, 1995, p. 13).

Teaching PAF 121 allowed me to understand the benefits of teaching learning community students, though the program would likely have benefited from the involvement a faculty member as well. Because of the residential component, the students established a rapport and sense of trust with each other prior to the first day of class, which allowed for a trusting classroom environment. Their bond was so great that I found it challenging to become as well-acquainted with the students as they were with each other, and I sometimes had difficultly keeping side conversations to a minimum. Yet, the trusting and comfortable environment encouraged students to speak up and contribute to classroom discussions. I appreciated the opportunity to practice a learning pedagogy that enabled me to use strategies such as reflection and practical experiences to help students construct knowledge and make meaning of their experiences. With only six weeks to teach the curriculum, it helped to practice a learning paradigm that encouraged construction of knowledge both inside the classroom and in the residential community.

Ball State University: Freshman Connections Program

Ball State University, along with many other institutions, has sought to improve the quality of its undergraduate program. To this end, administrators and faculty created partnerships outside the classroom in the belief that learning occurs not only in classrooms, but in all aspects of campus life. They hoped that interaction between students and faculty outside the classroom would compliment classroom work, creating a seamless learning environment. The Freshman Connections program is one learning community that grew from this effort. The program's success is attributable, in part, to its adherence to the seven principles for good practice to ensure quality undergraduate education described by Arthur Chickering and Zelda Gamson (1994, p. 255):

1. Encourage contacts between students and faculty.
2. Develop reciprocity and cooperation among students.
3. Use active learning techniques.
4. Give prompt feedback.
5. Emphasize time on task.
6. Communicate high expectations.
7. Respect diverse talents and ways of learning.

The Freshman Connections program strives to connect first-year students through academic and co-curricular experiences. Administrators put a support team in place to ensure the success of this program. The team was comprised of the faculty who taught the connected course, the students' academic advisor, and the residence director of the building. Additionally, one upper-class student was appointed to serve as the Freshman Connections Assistant (FCA). The FCA lived in the first-year hall and worked with the residence director to create programming that met the needs of first-year students. This position gave administrators an important student perspective.

Joshua Lawrie worked with a Freshman Connections program, also known as the InterNation program, as a graduate student at Ball State University. This particular program's focus was to connect American students with inter-national students. The connection was created by mixing international students with American students in the same building. The program was unique in that the entire residence hall, which housed 130 students, participated in InterNation; many learning communities only consist of one or two floors. The year Lawrie worked with the program there were only about 25 international students living in the building. The rest of the students were from the United States and were predominately first-year students. The following are Lawrie's reflections on his experience working with the Freshman Connections program and on the ways in which the program adhered to Chickering and Gamson's seven principles.

Encourage Contacts Between Faculty and Students

The Freshman Connections program encouraged contact among faculty, administrators, and students in myriad ways. Participating students were required to take at least two classes together and live in the same residence hall. Some faculty members who taught the required classes chose to hold office hours in the residence halls, encouraging students to interact with them less formally. This also allowed the faculty to meet with students in their environment, helping to break down some of the traditional barriers for students between their in- and out-of-class experiences.

The residence life staff also encouraged students to connect with their faculty through the Freshman Connections Assistant. The FCA met individually with students to explore their adjustment to college. The FCA then encouraged students to seek out their professors whenever they needed additional assistance. This position was valuable to the success of the programs in that the FCA could relate to the participants on a student level and bring that perspective to the faculty members and administrators.

As the residence hall director, I also played a role in facilitating student–faculty communication. I often attended the classes that were linked to the program in my building, sometimes helping the professor teach particular lessons. This partnership between faculty and myself enabled students to understand that what happened in the classroom did not happen in a vacuum. Instead, they began to understand how and in what ways their classroom and residence hall experiences were fluid.

Develop Reciprocity and Cooperation Among Students

The second principle—that of reciprocity and cooperation among students—is one the Freshman Connections program embodied. This was made easier by the fact that all the students lived together and took common classes. The arrangement encouraged personal discussions among students. It also allowed faculty and staff to bring programs to the students. The residence life staff, along with faculty, created study sessions in the residence halls and faculty held review sessions for tests in the buildings. The students were also connected by participating in a shared reading over the summer before they arrived on campus. This reading program was then integrated into the residence halls (i.e., programs, bulletin boards, conversations), and into the classroom (papers, projects, presentations).

Use Active Learning Techniques

The Freshman Connections program also used active learning techniques to improve the quality of education. First, we brought guest lecturers to the residence halls. These lectures focused on topics relevant to the students' coursework. The FCA then followed up with small discussion groups on the floors to get student actively engaged in the material.

As residence hall director, I also helped create an environment in which active learning flourished. For example, when the students were studying different cultures in one of their connected courses, the idea emerged for an international dinner. The FCA, several students, and I worked with dining services to offer a meal that incorporated various ethnic foods. This project allowed students to take what they were studying in the classroom and actively connect the material in a real-world setting.

Give Prompt Feedback

The Freshman Connections program was structured to give prompt feedback to students through the in-house office hours held by both faculty and academic advisors. The faculty office hours allowed students to seek timely feedback on projects and papers. Office hours held in the residence halls by an academic advisor gave students convenient access to guidance and advice at registration time.

Prompt feedback also came in the form of mid-term progress reports. I received these reports and handed them out to the students. If a student earned lower than a C in a course, he or she met with me one-on-one. During the meeting, the student and I would explore reasons why she or he was not doing well in the particular class. I also served as a referral agent if the student had questions that could not be answered during the meeting. This strategy of having residence life staff members serve as informal academic advisors was another way to create a seamless learning environment for students. After these meetings, students were more likely to have discussions with residence life staff about what they were learning in their classes and where they might need support.

Emphasize Time on Task

The Freshman Connections Assistant focused a great deal of attention on creating environments that promoted time on task. In the beginning of the year, the FCA held programs on time management and study skills in which students learned about the importance of using their time wisely during college. The FCA also coordinated with other offices (such as the Writing Center) to conduct workshops for students living in the Freshman Connections program. These workshops focused on the importance of college success skills. I tried to encourage students to study early for exams by holding review sessions at least one week in advance in the residence hall. These reviews discouraged students from cramming for tests, teaching them to use their time wisely for their academic benefit.

Communicate High Expectations

The Freshman Connections program communicated high expectations of participants from the moment they arrived on campus. Through a process called community contracting they were challenged with creating their own living standards. During community contracting, students came together as a community and discussed topics such as quiet hours, visitation, floor grade point averages, and kitchen use. What was unique for students living in the Freshman Connections program was that often their faculty assisted with this process. Faculty joined them during floor meetings and worked through discussions about academic goals for the community, such as floor GPAs. During classes the faculty would then talk about floor GPAs to remind students of the importance of meeting goals they set for themselves. This provided yet another opportunity to create a seamless learning experience for students.

Respect Diverse Talents and Ways of Learning

The Freshman Connections program encouraged respect for diverse talents and methods of learning in several ways. One-on-one attention from faculty allowed students to develop projects that reflected their individual learning styles. Students created final projects that helped them demonstrate their own ways of understanding the material taught in the class.

I used my position as judicial officer (one of my responsibilities as residence hall director) to focus on individual learning styles and interests. As judicial officer, I had to help students find ways to complete the requirements of their judicial sanctions when they violated the university's student code of conduct. One such instance involved a journalism major who had violated the alcohol policy. We decided on a penalty that involved writing a story about alcohol abuse on campus. After researching the campus climate toward alcohol, the student interviewed several students on the topic and worked with his professor to write the story. This project allowed the student to engage with course content in a way that made sense to him. This style of learning is in congruence with Barr and Tagg's (1995) theory on helping students create their own meaning by "whatever means works best" (p. 13).

Challenges to Success

Despite its successes, the Freshman Connections program did have a few problems to work out. The residence halls could provide no offices for academic advisors and faculty; they had to meet with students in the lounge, which lacked privacy. This was one reason a number of faculty members did not want to hold office hours in the residence halls. Advisors and faculty also had no computer access during residence hall office hours, making it difficult for them to use their time most effectively when they were not meeting with students.

The biggest challenge I faced was that students were grouped together on the basis of core classes and not by interest. Students also did not get to choose a particular connections program; they selected classes during summer orientation with an advisor and were placed in connections programs based upon their selections. Education majors might be placed with students majoring in architecture. This scenario does have its benefits, but, on the other hand, it meant the program had to incorporate an array of topics to meet the variety of needs and wants of these students.

Different Methods: Common Successes

Clearly, these two programs differ in structure. At Ball State students were grouped in a residential space based on class enrollment, whereas at Syracuse University the students were paired based on a mutual interest in leadership and then were required to take a course together. The teams that develop and support the two learning communities also vary in composition and process. Ball State's program has a faculty member, academic advisor, residence life professional, and upper-class student to support the program, while Syracuse University's program has an advisory board consisting of several student affairs professionals.

However, despite their differences the two programs share a fundamental pedagogy: both learning community models were conceived with the goal of enhancing student learning. Both engaged students in projects that allowed them to demonstrate what they were learning in class. At Syracuse University this was done through experiential learning techniques. At Ball State University it was accomplished through active learning techniques. While the Ball State model clearly defined how it created reciprocity and cooperation through shared classes, discussions, and residential options, Syracuse University accomplished the same goal through the LEAD community in different ways.

Both programs were successful in reaching the goals set forth by the institutions. A survey conducted by Syracuse University's Office of Residence Life asked students to rate their leadership skills after participating in the LEAD learning community. Students consistently rated their leadership skills higher then they did before living in the community. The community has also attracted juniors and seniors who want to serve as mentors to the program. Eleven upper-class students volunteered to serve as mentors in the community for the 2007–08 academic year. The demand for the leadership class was so great that a section was created meet the demand of the campus community.

According to research conducted in 2003 by Ball State University's Freshman Connections Office, 83.6% of students surveyed believed assigning students who live together to the same course is a good idea. This research also revealed that 66.5% of students participating in the Freshman Connections program believe that the experience helped their study habits. In addition to demonstrated student satisfaction, the program has had an impact in the form of lower probation rates and higher GPAs for enrolled students.

Universities across the country take different approaches to the learning community concept, but the differences do not necessarily make one particular program more successful than another. These two programs at Syracuse University and Ball State University are examples of the benefit of using diverse approaches. In one case, a residence life professional teaches a course and students decide whether to participate in the program. The other program places greater emphasis on developing relationships with faculty and staff to meet the needs of the students. Yet both programs achieve success in improving student experiences and learning.

References

Astin, A. (1993). *What matters in college: Four critical years revisited.* San Francisco: Jossey-Bass.

Barr, R. B., & Tagg, J. (1995). From teaching to learning: A new paradigm for undergraduate education. *Change, 27*(6), 12–25.

Chickering, A. W., & Gamson, Z. F. (1994). Seven principles for good practice in undergraduate education. In K. A. Feldman & M. B. Paulsen (Eds.), *Teaching and learning in the college classroom* (pp. 255–273). Needham Heights, MA: Simon and Schuster Custom Publishing.

Higher Education Research Institute (1996). *A social change model of leadership development, version III.* Los Angeles: UCLA Press.

Inkelas, K. K., & Weisman, J. L. (2003). Different by design: An examination of student outcomes among participants in three types of living-learning programs. *Journal of College Student Development, 44,* 335–368.

McKeachie, W. J. (1994). *Teaching tips: Strategies, research, and theory for college and university teachers.* Lexington, MA: Heath.

Schroeder, C. C., & Mable, P. (1994). Residence halls and the college experience: Past and present. In C. C. Schroeder, P. Mable et al. (Eds.),

Realizing the educational potential of residence halls (pp. 3–21). San Francisco: Jossey-Bass.

Senge, P. M. (1990). *The fifth discipline: The art and practice of the learning organization.* New York: Doubleday.

Stimpson, R. (1994). Creating a context for education success. In C. C. Schroeder, P. Mable et al. (Eds.), *Realizing the educational potential of residence halls* (pp. 53–69). San Francisco: Jossey-Bass.

Critical Learning Community Resources for Educating Campus Stakeholders

Terra Peckskamp and Joshua G. McIntosh

INTEREST continues to grow among college campuses in using learning communities as an institutional practice to strengthen student engagement, learning, and retention. Once administrators make a commitment to exploring the possibility of developing a learning community program, they are often challenged with fully explaining learning community philosophy, foundations, structures, outcomes, and assessments to various constituents to garner their support. This chapter highlights some key pieces of literature that can be useful in developing learning community programs.

Philosophy

Understanding the philosophical underpinnings of learning communities can assist in initiating conversations with faculty and senior administrators about learning communities. The first article annotated below (Barr & Tagg, 1995) does not deal exclusively with learning communities, but it provides a foundation for ways to think about the role of learning in higher education. The other articles are beneficial in that they provide a rationale for learning communities as a tool for improving teaching and learning.

Barr, R. B., & J. Tagg. (1995). From teaching to learning: A new paradigm for undergraduate education. *Change*, *27*(6), 12–25.

This article discusses a paradigm shift in higher education that supports learning communities as an institutional practice. Institutions of higher education have historically existed to provide instruction (Instruction Paradigm), but are now shifting to become learning-centered (Learning

Paradigm). Learning communities are one of many practices that support the learning-centered approach to education because they are intended to *engage* students in course content, there is a shared responsibility for learning between peers and instructors, and they are often interdisciplinary by design.

Cross, K. P. (1998). Why learning communities? Why now? *About Campus, 3* (3), 4–11.

Recognizing that some administrators view learning communities as simply a fad, Cross provides an overview of the philosophy and research that helps frame the reasons so many administrators and faculty members are interested in implementing them. Specifically, Cross argues that there are three categories of reasons for the growing interest in learning communities: philosophical (learning communities align with the changing philosophy of knowledge), research (learning communities align with what research indicates about learning), and pragmatic (learning communities work).

Tinto, V. (2000). Learning better together: The impact of learning communities on student success in higher education. *Journal of Institutional Research 9*(1), 48–53. Retrieved June 23, 2010, from http://www.aair.org.au/jir/May00/Tinto.pdf

In this article, Tinto argues that although the content of learning communities can vary widely, all learning communities have three things in common: shared knowledge, shared knowing, and shared responsibility. This article also shares information on the concept of co-enrollment to help readers understand what an ideal learning community should reflect. Understanding the philosophical underpinnings of learning communities can assist in initiating conversations with faculty and senior administrators about learning communities.

Foundations and Structures

The following resources all provide practical information on the logistics of implementing learning communities while also providing historical, philosophical, and assessment-related information. Learning community staff members have used information from these works to develop support for learning community programs, to influence campus climates, to deepen partnerships, to provide an overview to campus stakeholders who should be involved in learning community administration, and as part of faculty–staff development workshops that help create common goals and a common language.

Gabelnick, F., MacGregor, J., Matthews, R. S., & Smith, B. L. (1990). *Learning communities: Creating connections among students, faculty, and disciplines.* New Directions for Teaching and Learning, 41. San Francisco: Jossey-Bass.

This publication is one of the foundational pieces of learning community literature. Ideas and information on how to design, implement, and evaluate learning communities are placed within a context of educational theory and reform.

Laufgraben, J. L., & Shapiro, N. S. (2004). *Sustaining and improving learning communities.* San Francisco: Jossey-Bass.

This book, considered a follow-up to *Creating learning communities: A practical guide to winning support, organizing for change, and implementing programs* (Shapiro & Levine, 1999), checks in with learning communities on a national level and examines the progress made by those that have moved from learning community implementation to learning community sustainability. Areas examined include goals, assessment, and the experiences of students and faculty, as well as some of the innovations in learning community structures and uses (e.g., diversity education).

Lenning, O. T., & Ebbers, L. H. (1999). *The powerful potential of learning communities: Improving education for the future* (ASHE-ERIC Higher Education Report, Vol. 26, No. 6). Washington, DC: The Graduate School of Education and Human Development, George Washington University.

This valuable publication provides a strong overview of some of the different types of learning communities and also discusses the future of learning communities, including virtual learning communities.

Shapiro, N. S., & Levine, J. H. (1999). *Creating learning communities: A practical guide to winning support, organizing for change, and implementing programs.* San Francisco: Jossey Bass.

This book can be considered a "how-to" guide for implementing learning communities. The authors begin with the theoretical background and rationale for learning communities and proceed to curriculum development, reward systems, and administrative structures. The book ends with information on evaluating and assessing learning communities.

Smith, B. L., MacGregor, J., Matthews, R. S., & Gabelnick, F. (2004). *Learning communities: Reforming undergraduate education.* San Francisco: Jossey-Bass.

As one of the more recent publications on learning communities, this book provides up-to-date information on learning community structures, implementation, evaluation, and assessment. The authors pay particular attention to learning communities as instruments for reforming undergraduate education and improving educational efforts for underprepared students.

Zeller, W. J., James, P., and Klippenstein, S. (2002). The residential nexus: A focus on student learning. *Talking Stick, 19*(6), 7–16.

Updating a 1994 document prepared by the Association of College and University Housing Officers–International (ACUHO–I), this overview of trends, research, and current issues indicates how housing and residence life professionals can contribute to students' learning.

Outcomes and Assessment

These articles provide assessment data that can help administrators and faculty understand the positive outcomes of learning community participation. External information on assessment and outcomes is particularly important when developing support for learning communities. As any learning community program develops, assessment and outcomes data specific to that particular program becomes important for sustaining and strengthening the program.

Inkelas, K. K., & Weisman, J. L. (2003). Different by design: An examination of student outcomes among participants in three types of living-learning programs. *Journal of College Student Development, 44*, 335–368.

Residence-based (living-learning) programs have been understudied relative to other types of learning communities. This study examines student experiences and outcomes across three broad types of living-learning communities and compares them with a control sample at one university. Participants in living-learning programs show stronger positive outcomes on all dependent measures than the control group, and the strongest outcomes on dependent measures that most closely parallel the emphases of each particular program type. These findings can help colleges and universities decide which type of program best suits their needs, as well as which elements from the different types of living-learning communities could profitably be incorporated into the college experience of all students.

Love, A. G. (1999). What are learning communities? In J. H. Levine (Ed.), *Learning communities: New structures, new partnerships for learning* (pp. 1–8). Columbia: National Resource Center for the First-

Year Experience and Students and Transition, University of South Carolina.

Defining learning communities can be difficult given the complexity of the varied learning community structures employed at institutions of higher education. This article provides an overview of the nine pivotal characteristics of learning communities, highlighting the positive outcomes of their implementation. In addition, the article provides a brief but helpful overview of the learning community movement and its philosophical groundings (e.g., Dewey).

Pike, G. R. (1999). The effects of residential learning communities and traditional residential living arrangements on educational gains during the first year of college. *Journal of College Student Development, 40*(3), 269–284.

This study compares the experiences of first-year students in residential learning communities and in traditional residence hall settings at the same institution. Using the College Student Experiences Questionnaire (CSEQ), Pike finds that students in residential learning environments have significantly higher levels of involvement and interaction, supporting their intellectual development and integration into college life.

Zhao, C.-M., & Kuh, G. D. (2004). Adding value: Learning communities and student engagement. *Research in Higher Education, 45*(2), 115–138.

This article is a summary of a study that examines connections between student engagement (as measured by the National Survey of Student Engagement) and learning community participation. The authors found that learning community participation is positively linked to student engagement. This article could be helpful to those who are interested in garnering a better understanding of student engagement or those interested in assessing the effectiveness of their institution's learning communities from an engagement perspective.

Useful Web Resources

In addition to the print resources listed above, there are also several Web-based resources on learning communities:

The National Study of Living-Learning Programs Web site provides information and results of the first national study of living-learning programs.

http://www.livelearnstudy.net

The Residential Learning Communities International Registry provides a searchable database with structural, programmatic, and contact information for registered learning communities, as well as links to over 200 learning community programs.

http://pcc.bgsu.edu/rlcch/submissions

The Washington Center for Improving the Quality of Undergraduate Education at Evergreen State College offers a wealth of information on learning community implementation, structures, pedagogy, resources, and assessment, including a searchable National Learning Communities Directory.

http://www.evergreen.edu/washcenter

Living-Learning Communities: An Annotated Bibliography, by C. Ryan Akers and Merrily S. Dunn, is a comprehensive overview of many living-learning resources.

http://www.livelearnstudy.net/images/LLP_Annotated_Bibliography.doc

Afterword

Barry L. Wells

WHEN I began my career in student affairs in the 1970s, a cultural shift in higher education was going at full throttle. No longer were student affairs operations responsible only for basic needs, like housing and health care. At the same time, academic affairs leaders were beginning to learn the value of educating the whole student, inside and outside the classroom. Faced with the challenges posed by these new approaches, and while exploring the benefits such approaches could provide, colleges and universities began to realize the need for new ways of working together.

Across American higher education, a process of discovery, study, and adoption began, producing new ways of matching student affairs professionals with their colleagues in academic affairs. These partnerships have paid dividends for faculty and staff in terms of successful collaboration and professional enrichment. Of much greater importance, working together in this way is producing increasingly impressive results in the recruitment, retention, learning, and citizenship development of students.

To understand this sea change, it might help to consider the research of Richard J. Light, the Walter H. Gale Professor of Education at Harvard University. His work has been influential to the thinking of student affairs and academic affairs professionals at Syracuse University. Of particular influence has been his book, *Making the Most of College* (2001), in which he demonstrates the importance of the outside-the-classroom student experience. Syracuse University's approach to its learning communities has been driven by similar thinking since their inception, and thousands of students have benefited from the synergy among members of the academic affairs and student affairs teams.

Of course, such synergy does not flourish without creativity and tending by its participants. To bring the best opportunities to our learning community students, Syracuse University's academic affairs and student affairs staff work hard on collaboration. From graduate students to the executive level, we find

115

creative ways to share ideas with each other; invest the time in collaborative settings needed to build strong, trusting relationships; and act out our powerful, mutual dedication to continuous improvement. In this, our learning communities model the kind of engaged behavior and commitment to collaborative learning that we seek to engender in our students.

What are the results? In growing from two pilot communities enrolling fewer than 50 students in 1998, to more than 30 residential and non-residential communities enrolling more than 1,300 students today, Syracuse University's learning communities have earned national recognition, most recently by *U.S. News and World Report*. Learning communities have been cited as one of several factors behind Syracuse University's leaps-and-bounds improvement in student retention, and in particular its closure of the graduation gap between African American students and white students. First-year students are embracing learning communities as a critical part of the college experience, and many successful upper-class students and recent alumni are citing learning communities as one of Syracuse University's most valuable contributions to their learning and growth.

The results of these benefits for students, along with Syracuse University's continued institutional emphasis on learning communities, set a powerful example of how institutions and their students are served by partnerships between academic affairs and student affairs. As we embrace new challenges in the field of higher education, I am confident that our experience in the area of learning communities will help guide us to successful collaborations in a variety of areas.

Contributors

Nicole Zervas Adsitt is a doctoral candidate in the Higher Education Program in the School of Education at Syracuse University and serves as Director of Academic Support Services at Le Moyne College. Nicole is also one of the founders of the Gateway Learning Community at Syracuse University.

Eric M. Alderman, J.D., currently is an adjunct instructor at Syracuse University. As the Whitman Professor of Entrepreneurial Practice at the Martin J. Whitman School of Management from 2003 to 2006, he developed and served as the inaugural director of the Barbara Glazer Weinstein and Jerome S. Glazer Creativity, Innovation & Entrepreneurship Learning Community.

Paul Buckley is Associate Dean for Student Life at Andrews University and former Associate Director for the Office of Multicultural Affairs at Syracuse University. He is also a doctoral candidate in the Cultural Foundations of Education department at Syracuse University, where his work focuses on race, ethnicity, and culture. Paul speaks nationally on a variety of topics related to diversity, working with male students, college retention and student success.

W. Leslie Burleson is a consultant for the Office of Institutional Research and Assessment at Syracuse University. He is also a doctoral student in social sciences at Syracuse University.

Chris Calvert-Minor is an Assistant Professor in the Department of Philosophy and Religious Studies at the University of Wisconsin–Whitewater. He earned his Ph.D. in philosophy at Syracuse University in 2008.

James Duah-Agyeman is Director of the Student Support and Diversity Education cluster of the Division of Student Affairs at Syracuse University. He is a certified diversity educator, teaches intergroup dialogues on race and ethnicity, and speaks nationally on diversity-related topics. The cluster he heads consists of the Slutzker Center for International Services, the Lesbian, Gay, Bisexual, and Transgender Resource Center, and the Office of Multicultural Affairs, which houses the Multicultural Living and Learning Community.

jared halter graduated with a master's degree in education from the Higher Education Program at Syracuse University. As a graduate student, jared worked in the Office of Student Life as a graduate assistant, interned in the LGBT Resource Center, and co-developed and co-taught a class on sexual orientation within the Intergroup Dialogue program, where he served as a part-time instructor. These involvements, along with his interest in student learning and development led to his co-authorship of the chapter in this volume. jared currently serves as the Director of Student Activities at Washington College.

Sandra N. Hurd is the Associate Provost for Academic Programs and formerly Acting Dean of the Graduate School at Syracuse University, where she is also a professor of law and public policy in the Martin J. Whitman School of Management.

Jennah K. Jones is a Residence Coordinator at Duke University. She received her graduate degree in higher education from Syracuse University, where she also served as an Assistant Residence Director. At Syracuse, she is was a co-coordinator for the Leaders Emerging and Developing (LEAD) learning community and co-instructed a section of PAF: 121 Growth Opportunities and Leadership Development.

Jennifer Kellington graduated with a master's degree in education from the Higher Education Program at Syracuse University. As a graduate student, Jennifer interned in the Center for Public and Community Service and this work led to her co-authorship on the article in this volume. She currently serves as Assistant Director for Career Development at Ithaca College.

Joshua D. Lawrie is an Area Director at Eastern Illinois University. He is currently enrolled full-time in a Ph.D. program at Indiana State University, studying higher education. He received his graduate degree in higher education from Ball State University and served as a Residence Director at Syracuse University, where he worked with several learning communities and advised the Learning Community Activities Board (LCAB).

Maria J. Lopez will be graduating with a master's degree in education from the Higher Education Program at Syracuse University. As a graduate student, Maria interned at SUNY Upstate Medical University, with the Office of Residence Life and with the College of Medicine's Office of Student

Admissions. She currently serves as an Academic Counselor for Student Support Services (a TRIO Program) at Syracuse University.

Joel McCarthy is the Associate Dean of Students at Wells College. Previously he served as the Coordinator for Communications for Residence Life at Syracuse University. He also received a master's degree in higher education administration from Syracuse University.

Joshua G. McIntosh is the Associate Dean of Harvard College for Student Life. Previously he served as the Senior Associate Director in the Office of Greek Life and Experiential Learning at Syracuse University and the Coordinator of Assessment in the Office of Residence Life at Syracuse University.

Carrie McLaughlin is the Director of Student Life at Loyola University Maryland and a doctoral candidate in the Higher Education Program at Syracuse University.

Camila Lértora Nardozzi is the Counselor for the Spain and Chile study abroad programs at Syracuse University Abroad. She also received her master's degree in higher education administration from Syracuse University in December 2007.

Trina Nocerino is a residence director at Northeastern University. She previously served as an Assistant Residence Director in the Office of Residence Life at Syracuse University. She received a master's degree in higher education administration from Syracuse University.

Elizabeth Occhino is the Assistant Director for the Mary Ann Shaw Center for Public and Community Service at Syracuse University.

Heather Strine Patterson is an Academic and Career Advisor at James Madison University in Harrisonburg, Virginia. Previously she worked with learning communities at Syracuse University and Miami University. She earned a master's degree in higher education administration.

Terra L. Peckskamp is a doctoral candidate in the School of Education at Syracuse University and serves as Director of Residence Life at Syracuse University.

Jamie Kathleen Portillo is a doctoral candidate in cultural anthropology and a teaching associate at Syracuse University.

Braden Smith is a doctoral candidate in the Political Science Department at

Syracuse University.

Rachel Smith is a doctoral candidate in the Higher Education Program at Syracuse University.

Eileen Strempel is an Associate Dean of the Graduate School at Syracuse University, and an Associate Professor in the Department of Fine Arts.

Michele Tarnow is an adjunct instructor of sociology at Syracuse University and a visiting instructor at SUNY ESF. She is also completing doctoral studies in sociology at Syracuse University's Maxwell School.

Larry Thomas is the Director of the Collegiate Science and Technology Entry Program (CSTEP) in the Graduate School's Center for Graduate Preparation and Achievement at Syracuse University.

Silvio Torres-Saillant, Professor of English and Director of the Latino–Latin American Studies Program at Syracuse University, is the author of several books and numerous articles on Caribbean literature, culture, and intellectual history as well as on different aspects of the U.S. Latino experience. He is associate editor of the journal *Latino Studies*, published by Palgrave Macmillan, and editor of the New World Studies series at the University of Virginia. His teaching and research interests include the contributions of ethnic minorities to the national culture of the United States, migration, transnational dynamics, diasporic identities, and the contours of Americanness.

Barry L. Wells is the retired Senior Vice President and Dean of Student Affairs at Syracuse University.

Dianna Winslow is a Syracuse University doctoral candidate in Composition and Cultural Rhetoric. Her research interests include interdisciplinary approaches to writing and research; community engagement models and the ethics of service, situated and community literacies, scholarship and teaching for social change, and the rhetorics of social movements. She is currently writing her dissertation on the rhetorics and literacies of the local food movement.

Index